BUSINESS MULLIGAN

How to Give *Your Business* and *Your Life*
a *Second Chance* in a Changing World

By

Jeff **Martin**

Printed in the United States of America
First Printing: April 2016
Ver: 4/25/2016

To my parents, Dyke and Sally Ann Martin—for all the love, support, and mulligans you gave me over the years.

ACKNOWLEDGMENTS

Like any project, writing a book takes hard work, dedication and help from others. This book simply could not have been completed without the efforts, dedication and the help I have received from several people.

To start, I'd like to thank Roy Petitfils. Roy, you guided me through much of this process, and at times, seemed to work harder than I did. You continued to fight for Todd (my avatar) and helped me understand that I was doing this for all the Todd's who struggle silently with the loss of freedom business ownership can bring. I'll never forget the day I told you that I was Todd, and you looked at me, with tears whelped up in your eyes and said, "Dude, I am Todd. I need this book".

My wife, Katie and our three children; Ty, Matt and Ann Marie. Thank you all for putting up with me when I was trying to meet deadlines and make corrections. Katie, if you weren't such a great lawyer I'd recommend you become an editor. I know how hard you work for our children, their school, our church and for your clients. Also, I know that squeezing in time to make suggestions was a lot to ask. Thank you for your patience and help to make this possible.

To my mastermind group, The League of Excellence: Scotty Baudoin, Fred Reggie, Jeffrey Benton and Roy. Thank you for pushing me to complete this project and for listening to countless revisions of the Mulligan Method.

To Nancy Pile, Matt Hebert and Thomas Hauck for helping with the editing process.

And, for you, Todd. There have been so many times I considered moving on to other projects, but your voice has been driving me to complete this book. My love for small business and small business owners has become the purpose of Business Mulligan.

CONTENTS

PREFACE

If you know that you were meant to be a business owner, but have had a love-hate relationship with your business, this book is for you.

Look, let's face it—*a business isn't worth owning if it owns you*. We all have ups and downs, and we're all willing to give it our all, but in too many cases it takes years of struggle and hidden pain to realize that it's just not working.

In my case, I created my business out of thin air. It was my baby, and I was willing to do anything and everything to make it succeed. Like you, I got into business for all the right reasons. I am a bit of a control freak, and I wanted to be in control of my destiny.

A few years down the road and almost imperceptibly, the relationship I had with my business changed. I somehow allowed my business to go from something I owned and loved—to controlling every decision I made. It affected every part of my life. My health suffered, my relationships suffered, my family

> *A business isn't worth owning if it owns you.*

suffered, and at times I felt like I was forfeiting my life, so the business would survive. To say the least, that's not why I got into business—and I know you didn't either.

* * *

If I had a nickel for every time I've heard, "Life is short" and "You better live each day like it was your last," I'd have a nice chunk of change. What's funny though is that it often takes something to go wrong in our own lives to make us finally get it. And, when it finally happens, we're the ones who go around saying things like that.

A few years ago I took a trip to London with my wife Katie and my mother. They were going to celebrate an anniversary for an organization my mother is involved with, and I was really just tagging along. Both my mother and Katie had been to Europe many times, but this was my first trip.

As Americans, we always hear how young our country is, and when we compare it to England, for example, we are young. I was amazed at the art, architecture, and history of it all. I had a pint of beer in a pub that William Shakespeare was said to have frequented. Seriously? William Shakespeare died in 1616. I learned that the original George Inn burned in 1676, but one of the walls from the contemporary George Inn, in the interior of the structure that was rebuilt, is said to be from the original structure. The thought that I was standing where William Shakespeare stood rang loudly in my head.

I stood in awe of the art that hangs in the National Gallery. It's unfair to list just a few artists, such as Rembrandt, Monet, Michelangelo, without listing them all, but thinking about the artists and the subjects they painted actually living while they created these masterpieces hundreds of years ago took my breath away. I stood in front of Jan van Eyck's "The Arnolfini Portrait," which he painted in 1434, for at least ten minutes, marveling at the detail of shoes and dogs and rugs and windows and chandeliers. I certainly realize that dogs and rugs and windows aren't new to my time, but this painting left no doubt that people were really living full and rich lives in 1434.

We also visited the Tower of London. To hear about the history and see the buildings dating back to 1078 was simply mindboggling. Their structures are magnificent. Real, living people built them brick by brick more than 900 years ago. Every place we went had the same effect on me. Beautiful buildings and monuments built centuries ago by real people who lived and died. My mind was properly blown.

Nothing could prepare me for what I was about to experience at St.

Paul's Cathedral, however. Devastating fires were just part of the reality of the times I suppose, because like so many other structures, the original cathedral burned to the ground in 1666. Sir Christopher Wren led the construction of the current cathedral, which lasted from 1675 to 1711. Sure it seems like 36 years is a long time to build a church, today. But, I was and remain amazed that they were able to build it in that timeframe. Likely, tens of thousands of people took part in its construction.

As I quietly walked around, listening to the audio tour through the headset, I learned about all of the people that had worshiped there. I learned about all of the people who were buried there, in the crypt below the cathedral floor. And, a wave of emotions came over me. I guess it was a compilation of all of the places I had visited and all of the thoughts I had about the lives lived and ultimately died. I was overtaken with the realization that I was an active part of history. Of course, it was my history, but it registered to me that when tomorrow comes, today will be history, just like it was for all of the souls who had been there before me hundreds, even thousands of years ago. I realized that we are all just walking through time, exactly as millions have before us.

This is about the time when I would normally apologize for being so sappy, but this experience changed me. And, I want you and everyone else in the world to really get it—we get one shot at life. One. So, we better make it count.

You know how it is on vacation—you try to fit in as many sights and adventures as you can. We did just that, but after my experience at St. Paul's Cathedral, I woke up the next morning almost angry, and I knew why: I realized that I wasn't truly living my life. Sure, I had enjoyed great experiences, but in large part, I had only existed, not truly lived. I realized that my life was being controlled by my business and had been for at least the past ten years. My business had become a part of me, and I had given everything I could to it. My life and my business had fused together as if we were one, and when things were going well in my business, my life went well. When things didn't go well, neither did my life. I also realized that my business was not serving me; instead, I was a servant to it.

The more I thought about it, the angrier I became, and I began to harness my determination to regain control of my life. From that moment on, things would be different. I knew I had to figure out a way to do what I had thought a thousand times previously. I had to figure out how to run my business rather than allowing it to run me.

I returned to the United States with a renewed determination to recreate my business, so it would serve me rather than me constantly serving it.

My employees noticed an energy that they had never seen before. Nicole Patin was our director of operations. At that time, she had worked with me in three other businesses for more than 16 years. She sat down in my office one day and asked, "Okay, what has changed? Something happened—you're different."

I was different. That experience changed me. I felt as if I had finally awakened from a long sleep. And, I knew that if I was going to regain my control I needed a do-over – a mulligan. More specifically, I needed a Business Mulligan.

My hope is that you can have a similar awakening. I'm not suggesting that you manufacture a situation, but you should begin looking at the relationship you have with your business and assess whether it's healthy or not. Evaluate whether your business is serving your life or if you've handed over the controls to your business. And if this is true for you, take the time to figure out where and how you can get that control back— take that second chance, that "mulligan." These are all issues that I'm going to address in *Business Mulligan: How to Give Your Business and Your Life a Second Chance in a Changing World.*

INTRODUCTION

Technology is driving change at such a fast pace that we no longer understand our employees, our customers, or how our businesses fit in the rapidly changing world. We continue trying the latest "thing" because we know that if we keep operating as we have been, we'll get left behind. So, we constantly search for the "right thing," and, in doing so, we add layers of confusion.

If you compare your business today with the one you first envisioned, it's likely unrecognizable. Most technological advancements are designed to improve and simplify processes, but changes are taking place so quickly that it's adding complexity and challenges for which we are not prepared.

People are changing too. You and I, our employees and customers are all changing. We hear the doorbell ring and then the familiar roar of a large paneled truck starting up and driving off. We instantly know that the item we bought on our phone just a few days previously is now at our doorstep. In fact, we're positive because we got an email and a text message saying it would be delivered this very day.

The answer to our current challenges is simple. No, seriously— SIMPLE IS THE ANSWER. We need to simplify everything. Humans have a funny way of complicating as much as we possibly can. We complicate relationships, conversations, transactions . . . you name it, and we can mess it up. And, we entrepreneurs have a unique ability to mess things up. We throw a thousand things against the wall to see what sticks, and we don't appreciate that our wives, husbands, employees, and customers don't share in the fun.

It's time we simplify our businesses. It's time we take the advice that we've heard hundreds of times before—*Work ON your business, not IN your business*. The problem with that is that nobody has ever showed us

HOW to work on our businesses. Not until now.

It starts by looking at your business differently and focusing on the right things at the right times. I have developed a simple step-by-step process called the Mulligan Method that will allow you to gain more clarity, control, and freedom, so you can work on your business.

Before going farther, I want to define what a Business Mulligan is because I don't want you thinking you need to scrap your entire business and just start over—not even close. Ultimately, your mulligan happens when your business begins serving your lifestyle the way you originally intended it. And, that only happens as you focus on, adjust, and replay the most important parts of your business.

Merriam-Webster defines mulligan as, "a free shot sometimes given a golfer in informal play when the previous shot was poorly played."

Let's face it, you wouldn't be reading this book if you were pleased with how things have gone in your business. We all need do-overs in our businesses; otherwise, we remain stagnant and get passed up by our competitors. With that, however, I believe our mindset about mulligans needs to be healthy. THERE ARE NO RESET BUTTONS FOR LIFE. Golfers certainly aren't guaranteed that their second shots will be better than their first. Their goal is simply to focus on what went wrong, make a correction, and try to improve. This often takes hard work. Corrections and improvements must be made.

If you're not satisfied with the performance of any area of your business then focus, adjust, and replay. Focus on one part of your business at a time; make the appropriate adjustments, and replay it over and over—until you get it right. As you get farther in this book, you'll see that these are three foundational steps in the Mulligan Method, steps that we'll be exploring in depth.

I founded a DNA testing company before most people had ever heard of the term "DNA." When I first entered the market, in 1996, there was a tremendous buildup of demand from two to three generations of customers that previously could not get the answers to their family relationship questions because DNA testing wasn't offered to the public.

We were early adopters, and we experienced growth on a daily basis. To say the least, my business grew rapidly. I went from operating one stand-alone location in a strip mall, to selling franchises, then on to supporting the franchisees. That's literally going from one business to three overnight.

We also enjoyed many firsts: the first DNA brand to franchise, the first to have locations in cities throughout the United States, the first to integrate a custom, web-based operating system connecting all locations and customers, and the first to establish a network of more than 400 websites improving the customer experience on a local basis.

When I opened up that single location, all I needed was a phonebook ad and some swabs to make a living. The tests were about $600 and took more than a week to complete. Today, you can purchase a DNA test kit for less than $30 at more than 30,000 drugstores across the United States, and the lab fees are under $90. So, it's easy to imagine how much change took place in the DNA testing industry during the first 20 years.

I was forced to significantly change my business model four times. And, each time it was more expensive because it usually meant that I had to spend more to find customers and reduce profits to compete.

Does that sound familiar?

As you already know, change will always occur. How you respond to change can be much easier, though.

The Mulligan Method is designed to help free you from worry, confusion, chaos, and the feeling that you are so trapped in your business that you could never work on your business. And soon, you'll get what we all deserve sometimes—a Business Mulligan.

We'll start by introducing you to a new way to look at your business— in systems and parts rather than as a whole. Then, we'll begin to ask the right questions and allow your answers to guide your focus. Your focus will then produce the clarity, control, and freedom you need to work on your business and simplify everyone's experience as well. Your customers will thank you—*in the form of payment*. Your employees will thank you—*by actually working*. Your spouse will thank you—*as your stress level decreases and you begin once again to resemble the person he or she agreed to marry*. And, hopefully, you soon will love your business again—and your life.

In this book, you're going to learn the seven areas of your business that you must focus on, as the business owner. Each area is fundamental and required for success. And, although you may not be great in each area, your focus will allow you to ask the right questions, get the right answers, and regain control of your business and your life. Included are worksheets and exercises that I recommend you use to help assess where you are right now. Additionally, each relevant chapter concludes with an "Action Plan" to help you immediately apply the concepts of the chapter so that you can more rapidly transform your mindset and business to Business Mulligan success.

I intentionally wrote this book to be digestible over a weekend rather than weeks, but I hope you will use this as a reference to return to as you continue working on your business. It's extremely important to understand that results will not come overnight. I know you know that, and I just hope you know that your life is worth the work you'll put in your business.

Owning a business is great; however, owning your life is really the only reason to have a business. At first it feels overwhelming and that love-hate relationship you may have with your business might make you think it's not worth it—but your life is worth it. And, in your heart of hearts you know you love your business. So, let's get to work.

ONE

Kindergarten Simple

Businesses are like fingerprints—no two are identical. So, when some authors claim to know why most small businesses fail, they're right about a few things and simply wrong about most. Sure, there are similarities, but I believe that every business that has closed its doors did so for a host of different reasons, and no two are identical. One may have closed down because the owner originally decided to risk a certain amount of money, and when the money ran out, the owner was done. Another business owner may have realized that it wasn't what she thought it would be and learned that she preferred certainty and a steady paycheck. And, some may have closed because their industry changed so dramatically and quickly that the owners didn't want to change or felt that they couldn't keep up with the times.

We are living in one of the most exciting times that has ever existed for business owners. But, these times can also be brutal because we are being challenged to evolve more and faster than ever before. In working with business owners over the last decade, I have come to believe that most of the people who have decided to get out of business have done so due to their unwillingness or inability to continuously evolve with the times.

These changes can be overwhelming and lead to confusion. Ultimately the demands and pressures they put on the owners completely take control over their lives. Soon, their health, relationships, family, and productivity all suffer and can spiral out of control.

The last two decades have seen the most magnificent improvements in technology. For purposes of this book, technology includes: the Internet, computers, smartphones, and all the innovated applications that have been discovered that advance "technology."

Think about this: apps are now replacing entire businesses and taking over industries. Uber, for example, is changing the way people commute. Simply download the app to your smartphone and set up your Uber account. When you need a ride, open the app and choose the type of vehicle you would prefer. The nearest driver is notified, your GPS coordinates are stored, your route is calculated, and your fare is estimated. Once your driver accepts, you are given an estimate of when he'll arrive, his name and picture, the make, model, and color of his car, and his license plate number. You will see (turn by turn) exactly where they are located on a map and a countdown timer, as they get closer. Once your trip is completed, your credit card gets charged, your driver gets paid, Uber gets paid, and everyone is happy. If you have other Uber customers riding with you, simply press a button and split the cost of the trip. Within a few minutes, you'll receive an email with all the details of your trip, including your pick-up and arrival times, number of miles, number of minutes, a map detailing the route you traveled, and the amount you paid. WHAT!?!?!

Yes, the Times They Are A-Changin'

It's really hard to conceive, but again, a mobile phone application is completely changing an entire industry. And, Uber is just one example.

Regardless of the industry, technology is evolving by the nanosecond, and it's changing the way business is done today. It's changing the way our customers buy things and how we deliver our goods and services to them. Websites, social media platforms, apps, mobile phones, video, podcasting, blogs, email marketing, and many other uses of digital technology are changing how business is done. We have entered the digital economy and simply put: *if we're still operating the way we were two years ago, we're on our way out of business.*

In an effort to stay current, we often try to find technology that we can use in our business, but more often than not, we're putting Band-Aids® on larger issues. We're pressured by the rate of change, stiff competition, decreasing profit margins, and the increasing complexity of business. In fact, people are changing, and I believe that it's widely due to technological advancements, more specifically—the smartphone.

As a society, our attention spans and patience are shorter than they used to be. We have become accustomed to instant access to everything. Almost limitless information and opportunities are literally at our fingertips. Our employees are often in la-la land

If we're still operating the way we were two years ago, we're on our way out of business.

as they stare at pictures of their friends in exotic places while they pout about being at work.

Our customers have become used to shopping online and having their items delivered where, how, and when they want. And, they can cause significant issues with a single social media post or bad review if we can't satisfy their needs immediately. It's exciting and challenging at the same time.

With all the changes in technology, competition, and people, we attempt to do whatever is needed regardless of whether or not we have experience or if we're not the best person for the job. We wear so many hats that it's a common joke among business owners to say that they are their own IT department, HR department, chief cook, and bottle washer. Next thing we know, our business is controlling every part of our lives, and we find ourselves in an unhealthy, out-of-balance relationship with it. We often end up in a love-hate relationship, and it's time we start loving our business again. A good start would be to understand our business again.

Simplify Everything

Our businesses have become so complex and overwhelming because we continue to overcomplicate them. We're constantly trying new things to keep up with the demands placed on us by our employees, customers, and competition. If you look at the businesses that are currently increasing revenues, market share, profits, customers, and value, you'll notice a common theme: *they are kindergarten simple*.

The fastest growing companies today have honed in on their core offerings, messages, ideal customers, target markets, and culture, and they have simplified everything. Whether it's an app that schedules vacation destinations or a quick service restaurant, it seems that companies today are moving toward offering one core service or product, and simplifying their offerings to it. They identify what they do best, and everything else is centered around that one thing.

What Are You Known For?

We all have a core competency—the one thing we do best. The service or product that is so easy we can provide it in our sleep. Too often we add so many other products and services that we lose focus on what we're known for. Now, before you decide to scrap profitable items from your offerings, understand that I'm simply suggesting that we simplify things. Identify the offerings that are easy to provide, profitable, and in demand. Consider if they are primary or secondary products. For example, Five Guy's Burgers and Fries is a wildly successful restaurant chain. They have identified that burgers and fries are what they're most known for. Of course, they also offer drinks, shakes, and a variety of toppings for your burger, but from their name to their simplified menu, it's very obvious they focus on burgers and fries. I doubt seriously that we'll be seeing salads and chicken strips in their stores anytime soon. Kindergarten simple menu.

I am big on clarity. While you may feel as though you are already aware of everything going on around you, the truth is that changes can take place slowly and quietly as well as quickly and noisily. Regardless of how it happens or whether its cause is internal or external, change has a way of confusing everyone involved in our business. So, it's time to move from confusion to clarity. In the next chapter, you'll see how my life was turned upside down when I allowed my fear of failure to drive me to do whatever it took not to fail. Every action we take and every decision we make matters. And, if we're not clear about our business, we will never make the right moves.

Key Concepts

- Technology is changing the way business is done today.
- People (our employees and customers) are changing.
- We need to simplify our business, so we can see how we fit in this rapidly changing world.

Action Plan

- Identify your company's core competencies.
- Determine which products or services are your primary offerings and which are add-ons or secondary offerings.

TWO
Playing Not to Fail

I remember walking onto the tarmac and seeing the C–5 Galaxy. It was the biggest plane I had ever seen. The cockpit folds up, and they actually load things into it from the front and back. It usually hauls things like tanks, helicopters, and even other planes. But, on that day, they were only flying a few Humvees and the seven of us who had volunteered to stay behind and wrap things up after the rest of our unit had shipped out.

My executive officer at the time, Lt. Mike Halt, and I returned the letters we'd written to our families and had asked the other to hold in case something happened. After nine months of deployment to liberate Kuwait following the Iraqi invasion, we knew it was finally over. The enormity of this plane allowed us to sit as far away from each other as we wanted—and we did. You see, for the first time in nearly a year, we could just sit and be alone, be quiet in our thoughts.

As I sat there, I read the letter I'd written a few months previously. I remembered exactly when and where we'd decided to write the letters. And, I remembered both of us placing the other's letter into our respective flack jackets. But, I couldn't remember what I had written.

As I read it, I noted how often I told my parents that I loved them. How lucky I was that they were my parents. And, I remember reading

11

how often I said I was sorry—sorry for not making it back. I was sorry for putting them through the stress of the war. And, I said I was sorry for flunking out of college and disappointing them.

I cried as I read the letter. And, for the first time in as long as I could remember, I prayed and thanked God for getting me through the war. Then, I vowed to myself that I would never waste another minute that God gave me on this earth. I vowed that I would never disappoint my parents again; and I vowed that I would not fail because failure is what put me in harm's way in the first place.

From 1991 through 2007, my life seemed like a blur. I finished my four-year tour of duty in the military. I graduated from LSU with a finance degree. I bought a business in Lafayette, Louisiana. I bought three rental houses, an eight-unit apartment complex, and the home I live in today. I expanded my business into two different businesses and bought another one in another city. I met and married Katie, and we had three kids within 35 months. Then, I sold all of our rental property and my other businesses, and founded a DNA testing business.

Our DNA testing business experienced immediate success, and for the first three years, our growth seemed unstoppable. We franchised and had operations in 20 states throughout the country. We were awarded "best new franchise" and "fastest-growing franchise," among other awards. And, in June of 2007, we entered into an exclusive, nationwide distribution deal with a lab in the new field of nutrigenomics, and we invested heavily in preparation for that.

I'm not going to bore you with all the gory details, but there were three devastating events within a 13-month period that should have closed the doors of my business. Two months after signing the distribution deal, the owner of the manufacturing company suddenly died of a heart attack. We soon learned that there wasn't a succession plan, so his business closed. Without a solid manufacturer, the deal we'd made was dead. We had already invested heavily in a Houston call center in anticipation of that deal (that ended up falling through). We had hired and trained new staff and were obligated to significant marketing expenditures. To say the least, that was an unexpected set back.

I made the decision to move our franchise sales and training to Houston, and we began our recovery. Then, when Hurricanes Gustav and Ike hit South Louisiana and Houston in 2008, we lost everything in Houma and New Orleans, as well as in Houston. And, our Jackson, Mississippi, Baton Rouge, and Lafayette offices were each closed for several weeks.

As I said, all three events were individually devastating and could have closed us down. Frankly, had I known then what I know now, I would have packed it in after the hurricanes. But, you see, I'd made that vow 16 years earlier on that C–5 Galaxy: *I will not fail.* So, I spent the next five years, from 2008 through 2013, *doing anything and everything I could to save the business I'd founded.*

I cashed out of investments, IRAs, and even took the cash value out of my life insurance policies. I borrowed money from banks, friends, and family all the while masking my fear with a happy, confident face. And, I wasn't paying taxes in order to keep up payroll, so we could somehow sell our way back to success. I was working 10- to 16-hour days, and I was one hundred percent confident that I could out-work this challenge as I had done every challenge I had ever faced.

My wife would ask me how things were going, but I would only talk about sales—never expenses. Then one day, she got a call from a creditor, and I couldn't hide it any longer. She was blindsided and devastated when I told her about my retirement accounts, that I had convinced family and friends to lend me money and the extent of our debt. I was ashamed.

I could write an entire book on the struggles we faced following that revelation, but for you, these are the two important points:

1. She stuck with me.
2. It wasn't until that very moment that I realized that I had been blinded by my determination not to fail.

Every action I had taken and every decision I made following those three major events were made out of my fear of failure, not *my desire to succeed.* This was critical. And, this knowledge would change me forever.

As I began dealing with the truths of our situation, I realized that 25 years earlier, when I'd flunked out of college and decided to join the military, I had thought that I had committed to success. However, when the tough times came, I realized that I was more committed to not failing.

I learned that *there is a thin line between creating a strategy to win versus a strategy* not *to lose.* When things are going well, your actions and decisions always look like they were designed for success. But, when challenges occur (and they always do), your strategies get tested. I set out to figure out where I had gone wrong.

Decision-Pattern Awareness

We have all enjoyed success. There's no way a person would enter the world of business ownership without a certain level of confidence that usually comes from a history of winning or succeeding. And, we have all experienced challenges and failures. But, something drives us to tip the scales in our favor when we compare our belief that we will succeed to the possibility of failing. We believe in our winning over losing, our thriving over surviving. I had to figure out what went wrong. At the time, I didn't realize it, but my Business Mulligan had begun.

> *There is a thin line between creating a strategy to win versus a strategy not to lose.*

I started by listing every action and decision I had made over the previous 25 years. Of course, early on I recognized that my flunking out of school was a failure. But, I had a long list of seemingly good decisions and actions until it came to the challenges when that business deal fell apart and the two hurricanes wiped out all of our offices.

I created a spreadsheet and listed each action and decision on the left column. Then, I began to ask myself questions about each of those actions and decisions, and an obvious pattern emerged. The next three columns I labeled "Success Strategy," "Failure Strategy," and "Not to Fail Strategy."

Action/Decision	Success Strategy	Failure Strategy	Not to Fail Strategy

Of course, each of the three strategy columns were synonymous with:

Win—Thrive	Lose—Survive	Anything Not to Lose— Anything to Survive

I then thought about each action and decision I'd made, and placed a checkmark in the column that best described it. For example, I should have simply closed the Houston office, subleased the space and sold the furniture. However, concerned that such a move would be seen as a failure of the Texas branch, I moved my training center and franchise sales there listed my decision to move our franchise sales and training center to the Houston office after the distribution deal fell apart. And, when I asked myself whether that decision was made to *succeed*, *fail*, or *not to fail*, I realized it was clearly made out of my fear of failure. In hindsight, in that Houston office space that I'd leased to work with that other company, rather than moving my company there, I could have sold all the furniture and equipment, and sub-leased the space, but I'd decided to make the most out of the situation and avoid the perception of failure—both my own perception and that of my family, employees, and clients.

The same goes for my decision to fight our way back after the two hurricanes wiped out our offices. It was another decision made out of my fear of failure.

Again, there is a very thin line between winning and not losing, especially when you're in the moment. We often think it only becomes apparent after the fact—that that's when it becomes obvious that a decision was doomed from the beginning. But, that's really not the case. This decision-pattern listing process has raised my level of awareness in the moment when I am making decisions and taking actions. And, it has been instrumental in providing the clarity and control I've needed to fight my way back to success—that I've needed to have a Business Mulligan.

I'm sick of hearing, "Work ON my business, not IN my business."

Seriously, how many times have you heard that? *Psst . . .* Here's a little secret. I'm going to keep saying it. But, unlike most people, I'm going to show you how to work on your business. You can't have a Business Mulligan without gaining the clarity, control, and freedom required to work ON your business.

To help me use a similar consideration process when evaluating my current business decisions, this is what I did. In column one, I still have "Action/Decision." In column two, I added the word "IN" and in column three the word "ON." So now, for each action or decision, I evaluate it in terms of whether it means I am working in my business or on my business. For example, if one of my employees calls in sick and I take over their role for the day, that action is clearly working on the business.

The correlation I found between winning and working on my business is nothing short of amazing. Similarly, when I recognize that I'm working in my business, that particular Action/Decision usually aligns with "not to fail" (rather than "success strategy").

This process of evaluating my business decisions has been a game changer for me. It seems like each time I was doing whatever it took to survive, I was working in my business. And, whenever I made significant progress following a winning strategy, I had been working on my business. Admittedly, this is another thing that is easier to see after the fact. But, my level of awareness has been raised, and I make better decisions today, in the moment, by proactively examining my actions.

We have all experienced success and avoided failure through our willingness to do whatever it takes in our business. We earn respect from our employees and customers when we are viewed as someone who is willing to do anything we ask of others. So, I'm not advocating completely stopping all work IN your business. That's not realistic and frankly, I like keeping my "hands dirty."

I am, however, suggesting that you raise your level of awareness around your actions and decisions. As you begin to evaluate your actions and decisions, you too will notice a pattern. And, that knowledge will begin to shift your thoughts, and soon your actions and decisions will be guided by a winning strategy.

Recognizing patterns of the small actions and decisions of today is fairly easy, but as you will see, expanding this to longer timeframes, such as this past week, month, year, or longer, will be more challenging. As you do, you'll be reviewing larger events and each of them from a historical perspective. Hopefully, you'll see a pattern that will help raise your level of awareness about how you make decisions.

Business owners are always willing to put in the work—that's never a question. The question is whether it's best to work on or in your business. No one ever sets out to fail or lose, so as you make decisions, consider whether each decision is based on success, winning, or thriving; or if you find that when you work in your business, it correlates more with when you are trying not to fail by doing anything not to lose or whatever it takes to survive.

The responsibilities that come with owning a business are great. We are naturally willing to do whatever it takes, but when our businesses become so reliant on our being there, working in the trenches, it may already be too late. We own the business, and we need to drive the business. However, working in the business often leads to the business driving us. In the next chapter, you'll learn more skills, strategies, and concepts for ensuring your place in the driver's seat of your business.

Key Concepts

- There is a thin line between playing to win or not to lose.
- Reviewing your actions and decisions will raise your level of awareness around your decision patterns.
- Gaining freedom will allow you to work on your business more often, further increasing your freedom.

Action Plan

Whether you stop right now and take a few minutes or schedule some time alone later, please visit www.businessmulligan.com/decision-patterns and begin the process of learning more about how you make decisions.

- List your actions and decisions.
- Start with the actions and decisions you made today.
- Then, check off whether it was working on or working in your business.
- Finally, assign whether the action or decision was based on success, failure, or a not to fail strategy.
- Repeat this expanding to larger timeframes—this past week, month, year, or longer.
- Identify a pattern and use it to raise your level of awareness when you are currently making decisions.

THREE

Own It, Drive It

In today's complex business environment with its accelerated rate of change, what seems like a simple proposition—making a product or developing a service and selling it—can become overly complicated. You wake up to discover there are areas of your business that you know very little about.

Every business owner has experienced that horrible sinking feeling you get when a customer—perhaps even someone you know—comes up to you and says, "I really need to tell you that your employee who took my order was quite rude. I canceled my order because of his incompetence."

Or you've just received the first sample product from your manufacturer, and when you open the box, you think, "What the heck is this piece of junk? Is this supposed to be my product?"

Or you get a call from a vendor who states, "Your accountant hasn't paid us in six months. What's going on? Are you guys going out of business?"

Suddenly the areas that you have delegated—customer service, manufacturing, paying bills—now need your attention. You thought you could move on to bigger and better things, but then reality slaps you in the face.

One of the problems is that if you're paying a customer service rep fifteen bucks an hour and now you're doing his job, then you're doing a $15 an hour job when you should be doing higher value work (like a $500 an hour job). Your company is *wasting money paying you* because you're doing the work of an entry-level employee. If you spend your time fixing the work performed by your employees, you are not handling higher-level tasks, which are critical to the success of your company.

The question—and the reason you bought this book—is to learn how you can free yourself up from more of the day-to-day operations, so you can drive your business. It's a tough question because you need to accomplish three things at once:

1. Grow your company.
2. Maintain high quality and profitability.
3. Enjoy a satisfying personal and professional life.

Let's face it—goals one and two are attainable, if we're willing to work hard enough and make enough personal sacrifices. To accomplish them, all you need is a cot in your office and then to live there seven days a week, eating delivery pizza. You'll be a miserable empty shell of a human being, but, chances are, you'll have money in your pocket.

Living in your office is not an option—not for you, not for your family, and not for your employees.

The solution is to consciously build and manage your business *one step at a time*. This is the essence of the Mulligan Method.

Drive Your Business Like It's a Car

I'm using an automotive metaphor because most adults have driven or owned a vehicle. However, unless you're an actual mechanic, you probably don't know exactly how a car works. You know it has an engine and a steering wheel, and you need to do certain things to it on a regular basis to keep it running, like change the oil and rotate the tires.

You rely on other people to do the complicated stuff, but you also know enough so that if the mechanic says he's going to charge you a hundred dollars to change your oil, you will find another mechanic. In essence, even though you don't crawl underneath your vehicle yourself, your knowledge of how it operates is more than sufficient to keep it running and to maintain its value.

In the Mulligan Method, you'll see your business as a vehicle. Businesses are vehicles designed to get our employees, our customers, and us where we want to go. Each of us may be headed to different destinations, but we're all trying to get somewhere. Some of us use our business as a steppingstone to bigger, better opportunities; some desire wealth; some notoriety; and others want just a nice, peaceful retirement. Regardless, all business owners want to move from where they begin to a better place in their future. What that future place looks like and when you'll arrive depends on your own goals, needs, and desires.

Like most people, I'm no mechanic. I know how to put gas in my car and drive it but not much more. As its owner, I understand that my car has systems, parts, and component parts. I'm not a mechanic who knows how to fix these systems and parts, but I do know when they're not working and when they need maintenance. If not, my car will break or wear down to a point that prevents me from getting a return on my investment.

All cars have electrical systems, fuel systems, exhaust systems, brake systems, and more. You get the drill. Your car is made up of *systems*. Each system contains parts. And many of those parts have smaller component parts. There are sensors to indicate when something goes wrong, and dashboards to help us measure how we're driving.

On any trip there are potential hazards, potholes, detours, and other cars that can cause significant injury or even death to the driver and passengers if the accident is bad enough. It's easy to imagine that the car is our business, we are the drivers, our customers are the passengers, and the other cars are our competitors. Avoiding severe accidents allows your business to reach its final destination and not get hauled away to the junkyard.

It is imperative for you to begin seeing yourself as the *driver* of your business and not as its *mechanic*. This is the key to help you simplify your business (remember, kindergarten simple?), so you can gain clarity, control, and the freedom necessary to work on your business. I can tell you that I enjoyed many years of both success and misery before coming to this realization. Had I known this when I first started out, it would have drastically changed the trajectory of my success, and it certainly would have helped me avoid many sleepless nights.

You need to drive your car, not spend every minute fixing it. Put the tools away and get back in the driver's seat.

The Seven Systems

Just like cars, businesses are made up of systems. In the Mulligan Method, I've identified the seven systems that comprise most businesses. By learning these seven systems (and the questions that these systems ask every day), you'll regain control because you're focusing on the right things at the right times.

As the business owner, *you should be focused on the systems*.

Let's look at how your business operates in real life, every day. As the owner, you'll always perform some tasks yourself, like overseeing a new product or talking to investors. But for the day-to-day tasks, you need to rely on the performance of your employees. Your employees are engaged, minute-by-minute, with both external and internal issues.

It's your employee who serves the customer.

Your employee might be the one who interfaces with the manufacturer.

Your employee makes sure the vendor gets paid when the invoice is due.

How will you know if your employees are meeting your high standards?

There are three common methods:

1. Hear reports from employees.

These are typically given at staff meetings. This method is common but flawed because—for many reasons—employees lie. Well, maybe they don't always *lie*, but they generally want to present the best picture possible. Rare is the employee who will share at a staff meeting, "The project is behind schedule, and it's my fault." They blame someone else— usually a vaguely defined third party who is not in the room. Getting the truth can be next to impossible. Usually, the boss is the LAST one to hear the truth due to fear of angering or disappointing the boss.

2. Receive objective data, such as sales reports or product defect reports.

These reports are also standard, but they can be confusing and overwhelming. They can also be massaged by the people preparing the reports (see method #1, above).

3. Ask questions.

This method is often the most effective. For example, rather than listening to John deliver his report in which he blames the vendor in another city for being late, you can ask, "Tell me exactly how you plan to get this project back on track. Do we need to redesign? Do we need a new vendor? Do we need to call our lawyers?" By asking questions, you can zero in on the real problem and get your employee thinking and discussing solutions to the problem.

You've probably had this experience with your car. You've brought your car to get the oil changed, and the technician shows you the air filter. Of course, it is slightly discolored and doesn't look brand-new, but you cannot see any signs of damage or discoloration to the point that it needs replacing. So, you may want to ask, "What am I looking for—holes, dirt, bugs?"

Then, he tells you that your car's manufacturer recommends the most expensive synthetic oil available but gives you the option to purchase one of the six inferior, lower-priced oils. Before choosing, you may want to ask him to explain the differences and benefits of using the higher-priced oil. Or, the risks of using the lower-priced version

The point is that you need to know how to ask the right questions. You need to be the one asking and getting answers to the questions each system demands.

Let's go back to the systems. Here are the Seven Systems that comprise your business:

1. *Attraction* – Who? Who is our ideal customer?
2. *Conversion* – When? When do we ask for the sale?
3. *Delivery* – What? What value do we provide?
4. *Systems* – How? How do we operate profitably?
5. *Culture* – Why? Why do we do what we do?
6. *Administrative* – How much? How much do we keep?
7. *Personal* – Where? Where am I most needed right now?

In the chapters ahead, I'll show you how to work on one system at a time. It won't be overwhelming and you'll make steady, consistent progress.

To do this effectively, use my three-step process.

Name It, Claim It, Tame It

In many ways, learning to manage your business is no different than tackling any other problem we have in life. To solve the problem of business management we must use a maxim that's familiar in the realm of psychology:

1. Name it. – Admit we have a problem.
2. Claim it. – Accept that we have a problem.
3. Tame it. – Work through the solution.

Name It

Your car is making a strange noise, so you take it to a repair shop. The mechanic looks at your car and determines, "You need a new timing belt. It will cost you $500."

You're not sure if that's what you need, so you go to another mechanic. After looking at your car, he decides, "You need to have the computer reset. It will cost you $200."

Still not convinced, you take your car to a third mechanic. He declares, "Your problem is obviously a bad thermocouple in the fuel system. It will cost $400 to repair."

By now you're ready to drive your car off a cliff.

The first step in making your car run properly is to correctly name the problem.

Just as with your car, a problem with your business may not be readily apparent. Some problems are obvious, like a late delivery from a supplier. Other problems are not as obvious, and it isn't uncommon for a problem to go unnoticed until it has festered long enough to cause damage. Then when disaster strikes, you and your staff will be forced to scramble to identify and fix the issue so that you minimize the impact. Even if you manage to catch it quickly, your operations could suffer and even damage your profits.

How do you go about identifying a business problem so that you can deal with it as efficiently as possible?

By being attuned to your business by continuously collecting pertinent information about your business from your employees. You cannot depend upon reports. You can only identify the problem, and the design a proper solution, if you ask the right questions.

To solve a small issue before it has the chance to grow, you need to ask the right questions in a way that will identify the business problem and improve the area that's being questioned. An important part of identifying a business problem involves digging beneath the surface.

Beneath every problem is a deeper issue that needs attention. Too often business owners deal with the symptom of the problem and not the cause. For the problem to be completely eliminated, rather than simply swept under the rug, we must uncover the underlying cause. If you don't, you run the risk of the immediate issue coming back over and over again.

Let's say that you have a customer who needed to return an item that he purchased from your company. Somehow during the process the customer became unhappy, went online, and posted a nasty comment about your company's customer service reps.

You need to identify the problem by asking the right questions.

What was the exact chain of events?

Was the employee in question properly trained in the return process?

Did he or she carefully listen to the customer's concerns?

Has more than one person returned the same product?

Think like an auto mechanic who is presented with a car that's making a mysterious sound. The first priority is to correctly observe and identify the problem (name it). For example, when sales are low, very often our first response is to put pressure on the salespeople. We want them to sell more and bring in more revenue. But it's very possible that they're doing the best job they can, and the problem is in the product itself. There might be a problem with its design or construction. Or perhaps the product is competitive, but it's priced higher than comparable products from competitors. Or you may need to increase your lead generation efforts or fight to get better shelf space in the stores.

When you dig deeper, the cause of a problem is often never where the symptom shows up. If your business is going to be successful over the long haul, you must force yourself to look beneath the symptoms and find its cause and fix it.

Sometimes you may need outside help. After all, no one is expected to be an expert in every aspect of a business. When you need advice, don't hesitate to get it. It's possible that a problem exists right under your nose, but you're not skilled enough to detect it.

For many owners, things like accounting and taxes are areas in which they have little training. That's why it helps to get outside opinions. And I don't just mean paid experts; you can talk to colleagues in the same industry and anyone else who might be able to identify business issues that you could be missing. Mentors are good too—it's worthwhile if you can develop a relationship with someone in your industry who has more experience and is willing to give you advice.

By consulting with people who are experienced in parts of your business that you may not deal with every day, you can uncover and address issues that may otherwise be allowed to worsen over time.

Claim It

Imagine this scenario: A water main has broken in the street. Five guys in bright orange vests are standing around the gushing geyser, looking at it. A backhoe and other tools are nearby.

Guy #1: It's a broken water main.

Guy #2: A bad one.

Guy #3: There sure is a lot of water coming out of it.

Guy #4: Definitely a bad break. Worst I've ever seen.

Guy #5: The water's getting mighty deep.

Yes, these guys have successfully *named* the problem. But that's as far as they've gotten. They have not yet *claimed* it. Not one has stepped forward and said, "Let's fix this thing." They're all waiting around for the other guy to take action. Meanwhile, the water keeps pouring out of the broken pipe.

A common roadblock to progress is our propensity to wait for someone else to take the initiative. Too often at work we hear, "That's not my job or my responsibility."

People often wait for someone else to step forward. They think that Superman is going to swoop down and fix the problem.

But Superman never comes.

Ownership of problems starts with you. As the owner, you need to set the example. Claiming a problem begins with holding yourself accountable for your actions and how you do your job. Every day, ask yourself, "What can I do to improve results?" Once you've claimed the problem, back up your actions with commitment and keeping your word.

If your employees, however, don't share your commitment, your life will be nothing but misery as you run around fixing every little problem. It is imperative that your employees have the confidence to claim problems rather than dodge them. Some people call it employee empowerment; by whatever name you choose, it's important that when you're not around, your staff can function and even excel.

Realizing that Superman is never going to come can be liberating. When your people are faced with a business challenge, they need to assume that help is not coming. The responsibility is theirs, and it starts with developing a belief that they, as individuals, are accountable for the quality and timeliness of an outcome, even when they're working with others. Claiming ownership doesn't always mean they have ultimate authority over a project. Nor does it mean that they shouldn't ask others for assistance. But it does mean they own the obligation to take action and deliver results.

Claiming a problem can only be done in a culture of trust. Employees need to know that you have their backs. This means that if they step up and make a mistake while trying to solve a problem, they won't be criticized, either by you or by backstabbing coworkers.

There's a big difference between fault and responsibility. By recognizing the difference, you avoid the blame game and empower your people to take ownership of difficult problems.

A leader assumes responsibility for a situation even if it's not his or her fault. We admire leaders who step up in front of reporters and announce, "The problem this company has caused is my responsibility, and I'm going to personally make sure we correct it." We think, "Wow, there's a person who knows how to behave honorably!" We admire them. In contrast, when a company makes a terrible mistake, and we hear nothing from the leaders, we think, "What cowards!"

Often, as leaders we have to deal with situations for which we're not at fault. But while fault is backward-looking, responsibility is forward-looking. Focusing on assigning blame delays taking positive action and stifles learning.

By claiming problems—and encouraging your employees to do the same without fear of recrimination—you'll lead your company to new heights and free yourself from personally fixing every problem that arises. In this way you free yourself to work on your business instead of in it.

Tame It

Let's go back to our five guys in their bright orange vests who are standing around looking at the broken water main. After a few minutes, one guy decides to *claim the problem*. Bravo! He fires up the backhoe and starts digging. With great determination he digs up half the street. As the minutes tick by, he keeps excavating until the street looks like a war zone. The other four guys scratch their heads.

"What the heck is he doing?" they ask each other.

"Beats me," says one.

"Bob," they ask the guy in the backhoe, "do you know what you're doing?"

Bob glares at his colleagues. "Someone's got to do *something*!" he yells. "It's better than doing nothing!"

Well, yes and no. While doing nothing—that is, failing to claim the problem—is bad, it's just as bad to have no clear plan. It's just as bad to throw money or resources at a problem without knowing how to get and measure results. This last part of the process is called *tame it* for a reason. Anyone who's watched a lion tamer knows that directing the dangerous beast takes skill, sensitivity, and planning. You don't just walk into the ring and start waving your arms around. That will get you killed. Conversely, you don't want to kill the lion. You want him to do what you want. Killing the lion would be easy: you just shoot him. But that's not what you want. You want a nice, friendly lion that will roll over and let you scratch his tummy.

Bob didn't understand this. While his colleagues were delinquent for not taking action to fix the broken water main, Bob was equally misguided for pointlessly digging up the entire street. Both are extremes.

When a problem first arises, it's not always obvious how you can resolve it. Within any situation, there are usually many different actions that can be taken, and you may need to consider all possibilities that lead to the most effective actions.

How do you know what the most effective actions are? One way is to visualize the solution. The solution is your response to the question, "What is the result I want to create?" This formula can be applied to many different situations. Until you have a really clear idea of what you want, you could take a lot of action and get nowhere, or end up with the wrong solution.

One Part at a Time

You may ask, "How am I going to work on my business? I'm so busy surviving I can't focus on what needs fixing!"

When you look at the seven systems and ask the right questions, the answers will tell you which parts to focus on. You will quickly identify the one part that is in most need of repair. For example, let's say that on your retail website you've discovered that lots of people spend time browsing the products and even filling shopping carts. But inexplicably many of them abandon their carts before they reach the checkout. This tells you that most of your website may be fine, but there's a problem with the order form and check-out process. You tell yourself, "I can focus on my order form because my abandonment rate is through the roof. If I can change one thing, then that can change my business." It may not change the world, but small, incremental improvements can compound and make a big difference.

You don't say, "I want to improve everything by ten percent." You say, "I want to improve the conversion rate by one percent, referrals by three percent, repeat business by five percent, culture by one percent." If you work on these little parts, you can make even greater improvements in that they'll compound. Small incremental parts—that's how you change your business.

In 2015 there was an interesting episode of the *Shark Tank* spinoff series called *Beyond the Tank* in which Mark Cuban, one of the sharks, was coaching the owners of a retail clothing website, the Red Dress Boutique. He had made an investment in the company and was meeting with the married couple, Diana and Josh Harbour, who owned the company. The owners were absolutely convinced that to manage the company's growth, their entire website had to be replaced at a cost of tens of thousands of dollars.

In the show, Cuban appeared mystified and then annoyed. He told the couple that he strongly disagreed with their assessment and that the website was perfectly fine and only needed to be upgraded, not redesigned. In effect, he was saying to them, "Focus on those smaller things that really need to be fixed. Don't waste your time and money on something that isn't an urgent problem." It is advice that is useful for any business owner.

Now that you have a good understanding that your focus will be less about the overall business and more about individual systems and parts, it's time to look at the Seven Systems, one by one. In the next chapter, we'll look at one of the most critical components of any business—how attracting the *right* customers will save you time, energy, and money.

Key Concepts

- Treat your business like it is a car, and you'll arrive at your destination.
- You are the owner of your business; you need to be the driver too.
- There are seven systems that require the owner's focus and attention.
- Similar to life, to solve business problems—Name it, Claim it, and Tame it.
- Work on one part of your business at a time.

Action Plan

- A big goal to get you working on rather than in your business is for you to consider your business in terms of its systems and parts, rather than seeing it as a whole. To get you thinking about your business in terms of systems, visit "The Seven Systems" section of this chapter and answer the questions there about the seven systems at play in your business. When responding to the questions, remember—kindergarten simple. Be as definitive as possible.

FOUR

System 1: Attraction

Who?

Who is your ideal customer?

$75 Pizza

A friend of mine loves a trendy, upscale pizza place called Front Street. The centerpiece of the restaurant is a big brick pizza oven imported from Italy. While a variety of gourmet pizzas form their core product line, at Front Street they also have special items like fresh oysters. They also have a full bar with top-shelf liquor.

Recently my friend went there with a business associate. They had dinner and a few drinks. At the end of the night, the bill came to $75. My friend turned to his colleague and declared, "The guy who owns this restaurant is a genius! He extracted $75 from me by selling me pizza! Can you believe it?"

They had a good laugh, but it was true: Front Street owned the market for trendy, upscale pizza joints in that town. Of course, all around town there are a dozen other normal pizza places, all serving the same boring pizza. But, Front Street had a significant advantage: They had identified their ideal customer and owned their niche in the market.

Attracting the Right Leads

Let's assume you have an amazing product or service to sell. Unless you're selling water or a basic food item, you know that not everyone on the planet will be your customer. There are many reasons people don't buy good products—they may have no use for the particular product, it's not culturally appropriate, it's too expensive, it seems too cheap, it seems too complicated . . . the reasons for *not* buying can be endless.

But that's okay. You can still run a profitable business selling to people who *want* and *need* your product.

In some cases, your market—the people who *will* buy your product—seems very large. If you own a neighborhood pizzeria, you'll come just about as close as you can get to offering a product that everyone in town might want. That's why Front Street knew it had to attract a particular customer. At the other extreme, your company might manufacture a highly-specialized industrial component that's needed by just one or two big corporate clients. In this case, your market is narrow.

The manner by which you reach your target market is critical. Every company, large or small, needs to promote its products within its market. A company might have a sales team or buy advertising or have a truck with its name emblazoned across the side or pay a famous actress to wear its product at public events. All of these methods of promotion come at a cost, in both time and money. As the business owner, you must ensure that your investment in promoting your product makes a difference to your bottom line. Otherwise, you're wasting your time and money selling to people who aren't interested.

Attraction is not about generating leads. Attraction is about generating the *right* leads. A lead can be any point of interest that a potential customer has in your product. Someone may come into your store to look around—that's a lead. Someone may visit your website and stay for awhile—that's a lead. Someone may call and ask for information—that's a lead.

Business growth depends on a constant stream of new business, which originate from leads. Leads are critical to your business and must be carefully cultivated like fragile, young sprouts.

They also come at a cost. That's why identifying and understanding your ideal customer is critical. Before you spend a nickel on generating leads, you must answer this question:

Who Is Your Ideal Customer?

Once you can *name* your ideal customer, then you can *claim* them with your targeted marketing—and *tame* them with your products or services. Naming that ideal customer then, simplifies your whole business.

However, many business owners are afraid to identify their ideal customer. Why? Because when it's your service or product, one that you've invested time, energy, and money into, it can be hard to say, "Okay, it's realistic to assume that groups A, B, and C are *not* going to buy my product." You believe that your business can serve everyone, or at least a broad spectrum of the market. And you may be right. Your product may help everyone.

But even if your product is found everywhere, like water, you cannot market to *everyone*. Because in today's world—*if you market to everyone, you market to no one*. If your company is just starting out, you should only market to one very specific ideal customer.

This can feel suffocating. But generating the right leads happens when you define your ideal customer. To repeat, in order to *claim* them, in hopes of *taming* them to buy your product or service, you must first *name* them.

> *If you market to everyone, you market to no one.*

Here's the good news: once you identify your ideal customer and you meet their needs, they will tell their friends, and those friends will tell their friends. In this way, identifying your ideal customer will simplify your business as a whole (remember our mantra—kindergarten simple), which in turn allows you to work on rather than in your business. It's all about being the driver, not the mechanic—and in identifying the ideal customer, you put yourself in the driver's seat.

In this book I'm going to use the term "avatar" to describe your ideal customer. It's an interesting word that has several shades of meaning. Avatar was originally used to describe the worldly incarnation of the Hindu god Vishnu and was popularized by Neal Stephenson in his 1992 cult novel *Snow Crash*.

Your avatar is comprised not only of the literal facts of your target consumer—their age, what they like to eat, their income, and their hometown—but also what they *aspire to become*.

For example, a sixteen-year-old girl living in a low-income neighborhood might regularly purchase "Hollywood Glamor Lipstick"—not because she actually lives in Hollywood—but because she wants to identify with the wealthy young women who do. A suburban man who drives a minivan full of kids may buy a camo jacket—not because he will ever set foot in the wilderness—but because it makes him feel like he's connected to a lifestyle that's wild and untamed.

Identifying Your Avatar

It may take some time and effort to identify your avatar, but it's worth it. It creates simplicity and focus in your marketing efforts. If you don't, you will drown in a sea of options where the only swimmers who survive are those who have identified and marketed to a specific niche.

To identify your avatar, answer these questions:
- Who *needs* or *loves* your product/service?
- Who is buying your product/service *right now*?
- Who gives you positive or constructive feedback, so you can make

the product/service better?

- Is it a male or female?
- How old is your ideal customer?
- How much money do they make?
- What do they do for fun?
- Where do they live?
- How do they spend their days?
- Do they work? If so, how many hours a day, days per week?
- How much time do they take off work? Or better yet, how much time do they want to take off?
- Do they have kids? Grandkids?
- Are they married, single, divorced?
- What do they watch on TV?
- Do they have cable?
- Do they watch HULU, Netflix, Amazon, network TV, no TV?
- Do they watch movies or TV shows?
- What are they searching for online?
- Where do they spend time online?
- What apps do they have and use the most on their phone?
- What are your ideal customers' hopes and dreams?
- What terrifies them?
- What would it take for them to be happier this year?
- What's one thing they'd change about their life if they could?
- Why do they like your product?
- What experience does your product give them?
- Do they read? If so, what types of media? Printed books/ magazines, or ebooks and ezines?
- What blogs do they read?

Your lead generation avatar is your target customer.

You might say, "Jeff, I sell pizza! Everybody loves pizza! My avatar is anybody who needs to eat!"

Not so fast. While pizza may be a plentiful product, the pizza industry is *intensely* competitive. There are markets and submarkets and tiny niches. People are very fussy about their pizza, and a typical consumer may love one type of pizza and loathe another. Some people buy the cheapest pizza they can find while others will pay a premium for exotic ingredients. Some people want gluten-free pizza while others want high-calorie deep-dish. Trust me: no matter what industry you're in, you need to begin by naming your niche and your avatar.

Creating your company's avatar is something you can do for free or little cost. Most likely you have some of this data available to you right now. You just need to access it, distill it, and write it down. Give your ideal customer a name. Draw a picture of him or her. List all of these attributes and habits you have identified.

If you don't have enough information, don't be afraid to ask. You can do this through Facebook, email, your website, Instagram, Snapchat, and countless other tools available to either formally or informally survey your audience.

By the way, when you communicate with a customer, remember this ironclad rule of business:

Your customer is totally self-centered.

I don't mean that your customer is a bad or selfish person. What I mean is that your customer has choices and will choose the best product or service for their money. You do the same thing when you buy something, don't you? You don't want to hear a lot of excuses—you just want the product that you buy to *work*, and if it doesn't, you're going to send it back.

Your customer is totally self-centered.

As a provider of a product or service, your job is to *serve* your customer, not tell them your life story. Always remember that.

When you communicate with your customers, make it clear that your reason for doing so is to make their experience better. Sure, you clearly want to make your product or service better, but the customer doesn't care about your product or service. The customer cares only about himself or herself. They care about the experience your product or service gives them.

Because your customer is a person or group of people, such as a business, you'll never know everything about them because people evolve, change, and grow. So will your ideal customer. Your goal is to learn as much as you can about your avatar, so you can effectively communicate to them and in turn reach your target market.

For example, let's say you have identified your avatar as a forty-year-old female who has two or three children. Even if that's all you know about her, you know that she's probably on Facebook, Pinterest, or Instagram, in that order.

So if you're a restaurant, have a presence on Zomato. If you sell real estate in an upscale neighborhood, then you want to place ads in magazines that target readers who buy, live, or want to buy and live in an upscale neighborhood. If you send a direct mail piece, make sure it's carefully targeted. You're wasting your time and money by putting it anywhere else. Money follows eyeballs. Know where the people are. Know where your avatar's eyeballs are. And remember—it all goes back to simplicity. In knowing your niche and avatar, you greatly simplify your marketing efforts all the while maximizing their effects.

Your effort to reach your avatar typically starts with ads and goes all the way through earning referrals.

Meet Todd, My "Business Mulligan" Avatar

Todd is forty-five years old, and fifty is looming large.

He owns his business.

His business has six employees and takes in revenues of roughly $600,000 a year.

Todd's days seem to fly by, filled with fires that must be put out, while his weeks drag by slowly because nothing seems to get finished.

He has always been confident in his abilities, and he's willing to do whatever it takes to succeed, but his business is beginning to take its toll, and things that normally wouldn't bother him are now overwhelming him. His business has become complicated and demands more and more. It looks nothing like the one he originally dreamed of owning. His customers, his six employees, and his long list of obligations call the shots. His revenues have flat lined, and his salary is stuck at $80,000 with few prospects of going up. New technology and increased competition make it clear that what worked in the past does not work today; and for the first time ever, he isn't sure what to do or in which direction to take his business. If you asked him right now if he feels more like the business owns him or he owns the business, he would quickly tell you that the business owns every move he makes.

Todd is married to the love of his life, and they have two beautiful children. He desperately wants to be a hero to his kids and the husband and provider he thought he would be, but his plans to allow his wife to not work and his plans take his family on those great family vacations haven't panned out. He feels like he's failing. Most days, it seems that even when he is off work or at home, his mind is still back at the shop.

He's not sleeping well, and his health is beginning to suffer. He lacks energy and can't remember the last time he took time for himself. He gets the occasional break by going onto Facebook because he still feels connected to his old friends, but even that sometimes reminds him that he's not living the life he dreamed of when he decided to go into business for himself.

Like most entrepreneurs, he is misunderstood. Some people, even the ones he loves the most, have called him a dreamer, and some have called him crazy. They've tried to talk him into giving up the business and getting a boring paycheck job. But he knows that when he gets the right opportunity or has just a few things go his way, he will change his world and prove to everyone that he was right. His worst fear is closing the business and facing all the people who told him he wouldn't succeed.

He has found himself in a love-hate relationship with his business, and he needs to take back control, so his business no longer controls him. But today, he feels trapped.

Todd needs a do-over. He needs to hit the reset button. He needs a Business Mulligan.

Because I wrote this book with this Todd avatar as my target reader, I imagine that Todd's story greatly resonates with you, my reader.

The Voice of Your Avatar

Often, when businesses field customer complaints or requests, they synthesize the information. Most businesses have different categories into which the complaints are grouped and many have a FAQ (frequently asked questions) page as a first response to customer service issues. These pages are formed from groups of problems.

At my business, DNA Services of America, I started recording customer conversations and phone calls. We started listening to phone calls specifically for the language our customers were using. So if someone commented, "I need to really know if this works," we would write down those *exact* words.

I trained our sales team to use the exact same words, phrases, and pain points we gathered from these recordings when speaking with potential customers. Then I created ads and lead generation pieces using the voice of the customer as we heard them speak. Before we started this process, I thought DNA Services was in the family relationship business. I thought we existed to help people identify their relatives and ancestors. Yet when

I began listening closely, I noticed most people referring to our product as a "paternity test" or a "DNA test." No one ever said they needed a "family relationship test." After thirteen years in the business, we changed our terminology and, in turn, increased the effectiveness of our ads. Our lead generation and consultations significantly improved once we began using the voice of our customer. Talk about applying kindergarten simplicity to tame customers into buying our products!

These questions will help you to identify the actual voice, thoughts, and words of your ideal customer. You can use these questions when you prepare your lead generation and advertising messages:

- *In what ways does our product help you, make your life easier, better?*
- *In what ways can our product be better?*
- *What is one way we can serve you better?*

Message-to-Market Consistency

Your core message must be consistent throughout the entire process. The promise you make to the customer you're attracting must be consistent throughout the conversion and delivery process. This sounds obvious, yet I've seen so many businesses fail in this area. And it costs them repeat business and referrals because their customers are frustrated and not taking the time or effort to communicate their frustration. Often the customer does not know why they're dissatisfied. Perhaps they don't have the language for it. So they just fall away. But that's not the worst part. When they fall away, they usually take others— potential customers—with them.

You have to consistently deliver your message throughout your business. For example, we took the time to learn exactly what our customers needed from a DNA test. At first glance you'd think they need a piece of paper that proves that they are or are not the biological parent in order to have (or not have) custody of the child or child support.

What we learned through talking with and interviewing many of our customers was that the number one thing they needed was *the truth*. They needed to be able to trust the other party in the relationship because our customer was in a relationship that was naturally strained because of questions about trust. They were cynical about anything and any decision the other party would make because their trust had been violated by simply questioning whether or not they were the biological father of a child. They needed a DNA test report that they could trust. In their minds, because the other party could manipulate another company and falsify a report, it was paramount that all parties took a test that yielded a result they could trust.

Conveying that message was our number one priority, but we couldn't make claims in our ads that we couldn't fulfill once they converted to a customer. So, in order to have *message-to-market consistency*, our number one priority was to deliver results that our clients could trust. We had to say that we deliver results they could *trust*—when we were attracting them in ads, when converting them from leads to clients, when delivering our services and reports, and when asking them to refer anyone they might know back to our company. If we didn't consistently deliver that message of "reports you can trust" in every one of those areas, then our message would be lost.

If your number one priority is not communicated throughout your business by everyone on your team and by every lead generation piece you have, then your message can be diluted as well.

The alleged fathers could be ninety-nine percent sure they were the father, but that other one percent would drive them crazy. There were grandparents who couldn't hold their grandchildren because they didn't know *for sure* that it was their biological grandson or granddaughter, so they naturally didn't fully give their love in order to protect themselves. But once they had results that they could trust, then they could open their hearts to their grandchildren.

Here's a question: were we in the business of selling DNA testing?

The surprising answer is "not exactly."

Our unique value was that we gave our customers *peace of mind*. That was our real service. We just happened to do it in the realm of DNA testing.

The message that connects with your customer must be consistent from start to finish. If your ads attract leads with one message, then the message must remain consistent as the lead converts into a prospect and into a paying customer. If the message changes from one stage to the next, the customer's experience will be injured, thus increasing the likelihood that they will become dissatisfied with your product or service at the point of inconsistency. Dissatisfied customers will cost you referrals and repeat business.

You need to constantly and consistently communicate the same message in order to constantly and consistently attract, serve, and maintain your customers.

Now that you've identified your avatar and you know how to talk to him or her, you can customize your advertising and the tools you use to attract such customers, like Google AdWords, Facebook ads, website content, etc., to attract the right customers. You're also able to get in front of them, knowing where they live, work, and play. Only now can you drive them back to you as a lead and convert them to a customer.

Honing in on your avatar and your core message produces better leads. Converting your leads into paying customers is the next critical system that requires your attention. As with any business, the number of leads is irrelevant unless you can convert them into a sale, so that's what we are going to tackle in the next chapter.

Key Concepts

- Attraction is about generating the right leads in hopes of converting them into paying customers.

- You're not in business to attract everyone; you're in business to attract the right one.
- The right one is your avatar.
- Your avatar represents your target market.
- It's essential that your message to your market be directed to your avatar.

Action Plan

- Go to www.businessmulligan.com/avatar and complete the worksheet to identify, create, and locate your avatar.
- Go to www.businessmulligan.com/snapshot to identify the attraction channels you're currently using in your business and evaluate their effectiveness.

FIVE

System 2: Conversion

When?

When do we ask for the sale?

Rule #1a

We often focus on making the sale. That becomes our top priority - rule number one. For many companies it must be their top priority, because they don't have systems in place to provide other options. Our efforts to drive potential customers will only pay off if we convert leads into paying customers when we get the chance. Whether our chance comes in the form of a phone call or a lead walking in the door, this is our time to shine – our best chance to make the sale.

I've mentioned that the DNA testing industry was changing rapidly during its first 20 years. The early years were relatively easy, but as more players entered the market, price became the leading factor for customers searching for options. We began measuring what we could to improve sales and one of the first conversion points I discovered was closure rate. This is the number of sales we made divided by the number of calls we got, in a month. For example, if we got 100 calls in a month and sold 15 tests, we *had a 15% closure rate. This number became the Holy Grail for us.*

We believed that if we focused on our closure rate everything else would take care of itself. We set lofty goals and focused on everything that was involved in increasing that percentage: answering the call by the second ring, having a unique greeting, following our sales call process to the letter, asking for the sale. This number was our top priority for months. We intensely focused on increasing our closure rate, and although we had some short-term success, we couldn't maintain steady growth.

More competition entered the market daily, so maintaining a 15% closure rate was becoming a victory. But, I was frustrated. The fact remained that 85% of people who called us were basically rejecting us and we first thought they were lost forever to our competition.

Rule #1a was born.

We had systems in place to hold our position in the marketplace as we routinely closed 15% of our callers. So, we began following-up with the 85% we didn't sell to learn what we could do better. We soon learned our biggest lesson. We weren't losing them; they just weren't ready to buy at the time they called. Eureka! The answer was to be in position to win with the 85% when they were ready to buy.

We needed a system that allowed us to stay in touch and be ready when they became ready to buy. This became our next highest priority. But, it wasn't our second priority – it wasn't Rule #2. We had worked very hard and spent a significant amount of time, energy and money to attract those callers in the first place. So, those leads were still our leads. They were not lost as we originally thought; they were just on a longer sales cycle.

We had to develop a system to follow-up with and maintain the conversation with the 85% of leads who were likely to buy at a later date. As you continue reading this chapter, you'll see how we quickly raised our closure rate from 15% to 22%, increasing our sales by more than 50% within a few months and never looked back.

You can have a million leads, but if they don't *convert into sales*, they're worthless.

A lead represents a *potential* sale, but they haven't given you a penny. Leads who convert into paying customers have put money into your bank account. This is why conversion is the second of the seven systems that you, as the business owner, must understand and oversee.

Conversion = Marketing + Sales

Conversion is broken down into two different sections: marketing and sales. When you look at your conversion points, you have to separate them. Additionally, there's a further distinction between marketing and advertising.

Marketing

Marketing is aimed at your general market. Your marketing campaign may include many channels— social media, sponsorships, and public relations efforts. The general goals of a marketing campaign are to weave your company into the fabric of people's lives and to increase their comfort levels with your products or services.

Because marketing efforts may not directly produce measurable sales, it's often difficult to determine what return on investment you're getting from a broad marketing campaign.

For example, let's say you go to a pro basketball game. You notice that all the players on a team are wearing one brand of footwear—Tenny Shoes. This is because the Tenny Shoe Company has given the players free sneakers and may have even paid a sponsorship fee to the team so that people in the crowd, like you, will see the pros wearing Tenny Shoes. This will plant the idea in your head that Tenny Shoes are cool and desirable, so you'll be comfortable buying them.

Remember that when you see the team wearing Tenny Shoes, you're not given any information about price or how to buy a pair. All you see are five guys wearing the sneakers.

Was the cost of the Tenny Shoe campaign worth it to the company? The company may never be sure. But they know that they must have a "presence" on the pro basketball court. If they don't occupy that space, their competitors will.

Advertising

In contrast, an advertisement is designed to move your potential buyer from being a disinterested person to a lead or prospect. Let's say your target customers goes home from the basketball game and picks up a copy of *Sports Illustrated*. He opens it and sees a full-page ad for Tenny Shoes. The ad says, "To get your pair of Tenny Shoes, go to TennyShoes. com today!" He goes to his computer and logs onto TennyShoes.com, where he quickly finds the sales page. He looks it over.

Now he's a prospect. The advertisement has been specifically designed to encourage him to contact the company to make a purchase.

If he stays on the page for longer than, say, one minute, suddenly a pop-up box appears. It says, "Click here for a Live Chat with one of our helpful associates!" It's all part of the effort to increase his comfort level and convert him from a prospect to a customer.

When the comfort level is high enough, the prospect enters the *conversion point*. An example of a conversion point is when he icks up the phone and makes the call to your company. The business then has an opportunity to convert him to a customer, or you can make an appointment to go see him and the sales call becomes a conversion point.

Another conversion point may be the order form, shopping cart on the website, or anything that can be measured—shopping cart abandonment, successful transactions, phone sales, appointments, consultations. If you can measure it and it's a conversion point, then you can work on it, improve it, and objectively measure your results. That's the distinction between attraction and conversion.

Conversion includes all the points where a business could convert a lead to a customer. And each one of those points needs to be measurable and specific, so the business can work on that particular part. Just like in your car, there are parts and component parts in each system. One of the most fascinating things you'll find as you begin your Business Mulligan is that you'll rarely repair one part and achieve huge results. You're more likely going to see small, incremental improvements in many parts that when combined yield large results. Because the conversion system contains so many conversion points, it's easier to see how repairing one will lead to improvements in others.

Buying Temperature

Since leads are a source of potential income, it can be very tempting to put pressure on leads to make a purchase. While converting is critical for success, woe unto the business owner or salesperson who tries to persuade, con, or cajole a prospect into becoming a customer. While the hard-sell approach may work in the short-term, it will not sustain long-term business growth.

People buy when they're ready to buy. Every customer takes a different path to purchase. Of course, it would make it much easier to do business if every call turned into a purchase and if everyone who walked into the store bought something. But that doesn't happen. As consumers, we all have different buying patterns, and our satisfaction and willingness to continue doing business with a company often have to do with our feeling about our last transaction with the company, whether it was a casual visit to a website or a purchase.

Everyone has a "buying temperature." To explain what I mean, let's use the example of someone buying a car. Every prospect walks onto the lot with a buying temperature between 1 (casual) and 10 (hot, ready to buy). If they're at 1, you're not going to move them from 1 to 10 the first time you meet. It's possible to move them from 7 to 10 or 1 to 3, but if you push too hard, they will become dissatisfied and you will end up with an upset prospect on your hands. And we all know what upset prospects do—they go somewhere else.

You want your customer to

- buy your product or service,
- buy it willingly, and
- be happy with it.

Therefore, the sales process is not a matter of persuasion but a matter of education and making the prospect comfortable with the purchase.

Customer comfort is key. Comfort may mean believing the product is affordable, or is durable, or will match the décor of the house, or is made in America, or that it won't pollute the environment. Maybe your lead needs assurance that the product will be accepted by his peer group. People have a nearly infinite variety of "tests" to determine acceptance of a product. For example, if a teenage girl is buying a new pair of shoes, she may have only one required test: will her friends think they're cool? Her mother, meanwhile, may have just one important test for those same shoes: do they provide good arch support? Her father may have his own test: are they affordable? If all three stakeholders are comfortable, the sale of the shoes will "stick." The shoes won't be returned to the store the next day.

Conversion Points

A conversion point is that area or point of interaction between the company and the customer that results in the customer deciding to move from one stage to another; ideally leading toward making a purchase. For a typical business, there can be many different conversion points—your website, elements on your website, phone calls, call-to-action's (CTA's), opt-in forms, landing pages, free content, shopping cart, white papers, ebooks, talking with a salesperson, and engagement elements.

While it's terrific if someone decides to buy after the very first contact with your product, this rarely happens. Consumers usually need repeated points of contact before they decide to buy. They may need to see an advertisement, hear about your product from a friend, see another advertisement, read a review on social media, and visit your website before they decide to get out the credit card.

As I mentioned earlier, leads who never convert are worthless. You need leads to convert into paying customers at an acceptably profitable *conversion rate*. This is quite simply the percentage of *qualified leads* who become customers.

Have a Marketing Plan

Developing a marketing plan is critical to the success of your business. Without one you cannot effectively market the message you want to deliver. You need to develop a marketing roadmap or plan, and measure the effectiveness of the conversions. Unfortunately when you're working IN your business, you can't measure, react, and adjust because you're so focused on the tasks of its daily operations that you can't see the big picture, the plan, needed to move it forward.

A marketing plan outlines the decisions you make so that your marketing tactics are most effective—it provides a way to work on your business and keep you in the driver's seat.

Your *target market* is the particular group of consumers to whom your product or service is aimed. An avatar helps you locate that target market and find the voice your company should use to talk to the market. You've already identified your avatar, and you know where he or she lives, plays, and where you can go to attract them. Determining your positioning will help you to deliver your message and implement your marketing strategy to your target market.

A marketing plan for a small business typically includes:

• *Your marketing mission statement.*

Write a few sentences that describe your key market (whom you're selling to), the value you provide (what you're selling), and your distinction (your unique selling proposition).

• *Description of your target market.*

Who will buy your product or service? This includes your avatar and the associated demographic information. For example, in my business, through a survey of former customers, we identified that our customers fell in the age range of 18 to 29 years old. They were typically living paycheck to paycheck, and pricing was important to them. They were single and obviously had a child through a current or former relationship. They found us on their mobile devices.

Collect, organize, and write down data about the market that is currently buying the product or service you will sell. Some areas to consider include market dynamics and patterns, including seasonality, customer demographics, market segment, customer target markets, customer needs, customer buying decisions, competing products, current sales in the industry, and benchmarks in the industry. You'll notice that some of this data is the equivalent of what you determined in characterizing your avatar, but that's not true for all of the information. Although your avatar is a respresentative of your target market, the market itself is much broader than that on individual person.

• *Knowledge of your competition.*

You need to know how your products and services are different from those of your competition. What is the price point at which your competitors are selling, and what segment of the market are they aiming to reach? Knowing your competitors and their products will help you better position your business and fill a niche they may be missing.

• *Description of the product or service, including special features.*

How does your product relate to the market? What does your market need, what do they currently use, and what do they need above and beyond current use? Include suppliers and vendors that you will need to rely on.

• *Marketing budget, including the advertising and promotional plan.*

What sales channels will you use—brick-and-mortar store, online sales, sales reps, house parties? Also include a "red light" decision point. For each activity, establish a metric that tells you to stop if it's not generating sufficient return on investment. You have to know when to pull the plug on an unsuccessful effort.

• *Pricing strategy.*

From the information you've collected, establish strategies for determining the price of your product, where your product will be positioned in the market, and how you will achieve brand awareness.

• *Market segmentation.*

Market segmentation refers to a description of competitors, including the level of demand for the product or service and the strengths and weaknesses of competitors. What is the perception of your brand in the marketplace? For example, if your restaurant sells pizza, do customers see you as the place to go for gluten-free or healthy options, or the place to go if they've got an appetite for fast, cheap food? The difference in how the target market sees you is your *positioning*. It is imperative that you know how to correctly position yourself in the eyes of your avatar. One way to do so is to develop compelling branding and marketing messages that clearly communicate how you want to be perceived.

• *Description of the business location, including advantages and disadvantages for marketing.*

• *Marketing goals.*

Establishing quantifiable marketing goals that you can measure and turn into numbers will allow you to ensure your marketing dollars and efforts are being well spent. For instance, your goal in one month might be to gain at least fifty new customers, sell a thousand units per week, or increase your revenue by five percent. Your goals might include sales, profits, or customer satisfaction.

• *Monitoring of your results.*

Everything you do will be pointless unless you track your results and compare them to your goals and to past performance. Test, analyze, and identify the strategies that are working. Survey your customers. Track sales, leads, and visitors to your website, as well as conversion rates at various sales points. Test programs over the course of a 30 to 60-day period, and evaluate the results. Repeat any programs that are delivering sales or building prospects, and get rid of anything that's not.

Unique Benefit

Your unique benefit is what you offer the customer that makes you different from your competition. You provide a unique solution to your target market's problem that is uniquely different from that of your competition. If you don't identify and promote your uniqueness, you'll be drowned out in a sea of sameness and spend more time flailing without conveying your value to the customer. In the end you'll be working harder for fewer conversions. And fewer conversions mean less money.

Let's look at Uber again. Uber's unique benefit is time saved for the customer. Prior to Uber, you'd look up a cab company, call the dispatcher, and wait for the cab to come after its last fare, regardless of where that was. Uber saves you time by connecting with the closest available driver, resulting in you getting to your location faster than with a traditional taxi service.

In the case of DNA Services, we offered our results online, we provided instructional videos, and we offered to connect with the other parties to gain trust for our organization. We were talking to grandparents, alleged fathers, and mothers, just to prove to them that we were reputable. That set us apart from our competition.

Remember that *features* and *benefits* are not the same. Features are surface statements about your product, such as what it can do, its dimensions, and its specifications. Benefits, on the other hand, show the end result of what a product can actually accomplish for the customer. It can be difficult to tell the difference between the two, as many features might sound like benefits.

For example, a fast Internet connection is a feature, but the ability to get vital information quickly is a benefit. Saying that a cell phone has a fast Internet connection is actually showcasing a feature, not a benefit. A benefit of fast Internet would be the ability to quickly get directions when you're lost.

A key difference between features and benefits is that the latter provides an emotional boost that customers can relate to. The fast Internet feature sounds vaguely positive, but on its own, there's no quickly understandable reason why it's positive. Meanwhile, almost every consumer can empathize with being lost and wanting an immediate solution to the problem.

Getting good gas mileage on a car is a feature; the amount of money you can save on gas is a benefit.

Home delivery of pizza is a feature; not having to leave your house to get dinner is a benefit.

Having pockets on your coat is a feature; having a place for your keys and keeping your hands warm in the winter are both benefits.

Be sure you highlight the benefits of your product first. Only then provide the customer with the features that make the benefits possible. For example, say, "Never get lost on the road again! Always arrive safely [the benefits] with our turn-by-turn voice navigation system [the feature]."

Unique Differentiator

A unique differentiator can be defined as your business attribute and/ or unique value that clearly separates you from the competition in your target marketplace. A key differentiator should be *unique, measurable,* and *defendable*. It should answer the customer's question, "Why should I purchase the product or service from you versus all other alternatives on the market?

Again, look at Uber. Their unique benefit as we mentioned earlier, is time saved. Their unique *differentiator* is the location and method of the transaction itself. With Uber, instead of the lengthy process of looking up and calling a dispatcher, you can summon a driver with a couple of clicks on your phone.

To be successful, a key differentiator must meet three important criteria:

1. It must be true. You can't make it up.

2. It must be important to your customers. If not, what's the point?

3. It must be verifiable. If you can't demonstrate that it is true, it won't be believed.

Here's where operating a small business can be an advantage. Unlike big global companies, which tend to remain faceless and build a generic brand image, a small business like yours has a better chance of success if you focus on individuals. No one else in the world has the same story as you. Your passions, your values, your ideas, your sense of humor, your story is unique, no matter how many people invade your industry. This includes your employees, board members, vendors, and partners. All are special, just like you. No other company in the world has the same combination and that makes your company stand apart.

Make sure that your differentiator is one that can highlight the advantages of choosing your company over your competitors. At DNA Services, we started offering private online results, and before long everyone copied us. So we offered a peace of mind guarantee, where if you didn't trust your report, then we would recollect and send your samples to another laboratory, and if they didn't match, we would pay the cost for both tests. We never got challenged.

Making an offer like that requires knowing that trust is that important to your customer. That is a play you can never make unless you know what consumer concern you're addressing. And for our customer it was trust.

Unless you have a strategy statement, you can't talk with your market effectively.

Create a Sales Process

In keeping with the theme of "kindergarten simple," your sales process must be simple, step-by-step, well documented, and easy to measure. Regardless of the industry or business, a good sales process is critical for converting prospects into paying customers.

Looking at your sales process in parts is vital to improvement. Gaps in the process will become self-evident quickly. Your sales team should enjoy perfecting the process, and usually the numbers motivate these guys.

As you begin applying the Mulligan Method and attending to the parts within your conversion system, you will steadily increase your number of good, paying customers. You've kept the core message throughout attraction and conversion, so when you begin delivering value through your products and services, you want to ensure that the core message remains intact.

In the next of the seven systems, delivery, you'll see opportunities to create referrals and repeat business because of customer satisfaction, which comes through a positive experience resulting from you keeping your promise—by meeting and exceeding your customers' expectations.

Key Concepts

- Every lead has a buying temperature.
- You cannot force a sale. People buy when they're ready.
- Conversion is a process that flows from marketing to sales.
- The message you start with in the attraction phase must continue

through conversion and through delivery.

- Identifying and measuring your conversion points are the only ways to increase sales.

Action Plan

- Go to www.businessmulligan.com/snapshot and identify all of the marketing channels currently used in your business.
- Identify your sales process and how you make sales.
- Develop your marketing strategy.

SIX

System 3: Delivery

What?

What value do we deliver?

Fresh Lemon Wedge

It was my senior year in college.

Since we were both about to graduate with degrees in finance, my buddy Brandon Goll and I thought we had the whole world figured out. We critiqued every business we drove past. Brandon's perspectives were always insightful and interesting, but his thick New Orleans accent and demeanor made everything he said sound hilarious.

One day we went out to eat lunch at a local restaurant. We were enjoying our meal—the food and atmosphere were great, and the waitress was very attentive. Before Brandon asked for a refill of iced tea, the waitress poured more from a pitcher. Then she walked away. I thought nothing of it, but Brandon immediately turned to me and gave me one of his looks.

"Oh, boy, here we go," I thought. I knew I was about to hear a sermon but wasn't sure on what. On that day, it was on customer service.

"D'ja see dat?" Brandon asked me. (Translation for anyone outside of New Orleans: Did you see that?)

"See what?" I asked.

After a few minutes of ranting, infused with the occasional curse word, he finally arrived at the lesson and summed it up only as he could do.

He said, "Ya see, what the consumer wants is a fresh lemon wedge."

He was right. As a consumer, if I order and pay for iced tea, with lemon, isn't it reasonable to expect a fresh lemon wedge with my next glass of iced tea? Seriously, the original glass is fantastic. It has ice, tea, and lemon. If the restaurant offers free refills, shouldn't all subsequent glasses be exactly the same and include a fresh lemon wedge?

Now, before you think Brandon and I are crazy, test it out for yourself. I bet what you'll find is that better restaurants either bring a small plate of lemon wedges with your tea or they bring more lemons with your refills. Furthermore, I bet you'll notice every time you don't get a fresh lemon wedge with your next hundred or so iced tea refills, and you'll feel like the service could be better.

Regardless of what business you're in, you must design your delivery system to meet and exceed your customers' expectations. Whether you offer products, services, or a combination, your customers, their expectations, what they want, what they need, and exceeding their expectations are paramount in the delivery system.

Exceeding Expectations Creates Value

When a customer enters into a transaction with your company, they have formed a contract in their minds. For example, let's revisit our friends at the Tenny Shoe Company. The contract might be this: I intend to pay Tenny Shoe Company the sum of one hundred dollars. For this amount of money I expect the following chain of events:

1. I drive to the Tenny Shoe store at the mall.
2. I park my car conveniently and for free at the mall.
3. I walk into the attractive Tenny Shoe store, which, of course, is open for business, not unexpectedly closed.
4. Within fifteen seconds I'm greeted by a friendly and well-groomed salesperson, who doesn't pressure me. The salesperson says, "If I can help you, please let me know."
5. I browse the displays of shoes and find the model I'm interested in. It looks every bit as attractive as it did in the advertisement—the marketing piece that turned me from an ordinary citizen to a viable prospect.
6. I show the friendly salesperson the shoe, and he quickly gets a pair in my size from the stockroom. I try them on, and they fit perfectly. So far so good!
7. I pay one hundred dollars for the shoes. At the counter the salesperson gives me a free pair of shoelaces. I didn't expect that.
8. I take the shoes home. I understand that if I don't like them—for any reason—I have seven days to return them for a full cash refund, no questions asked. I also understand that if, for any reason, the shoes fall apart within a year, I can return them for a new pair. This makes me comfortable with my purchase.
9. In the shoebox I find a coupon for a ten percent discount on my next purchase. Nice!
10. I wear the shoes to the gym. My best friend sees me and shouts, "OMG! Where did you get those shoes? They're amazing!" I tell her I got the shoes from the Tenny Shoe store at the mall. My friend thinks I'm a fashion guru.

The Cost of Unmet Expectations

In this example, my expectations were met and exceeded. I will be a repeat Tenny Shoe customer.

Business owners must understand that during any one of the ten steps, my experience could have soured. Here are just a few of the ways it could have turned out badly for Tenny Shoe:

1. Driving to the mall, I encounter a huge traffic jam. I say, "Screw it," turn around, go home, and order sneakers from Zappos.

2. The parking lot is full. I drive around, look for an open spot, and get increasingly upset. See #1 above.

3. I manage to park at the far end of the lot. After hiking to the mall entrance, I discover the Tenny Shoe store is closed for renovations. See #1 above.

4. The store is open. Once inside the store, I'm either ignored by the salesperson, or the salesperson jumps all over me and makes me feel that I need to buy something *right now*. I'm tense and unhappy.

5. The shoe display is confusing. I look around but don't see the shoe I want. I'm getting exasperated. Plus, the store smells bad, like they've pumped Eau de Sneaker into the ventilation system. And the music is really loud, like I'm in a trendy discotheque. I'm getting a headache.

6. I ask the salesperson for help. He disappears into the backroom. He's gone for ten minutes. Maybe he went on a break? I ask another salesperson to find the first guy. She's too busy, can't do it now. I wait.

7. Finally I get the shoes. I pay one hundred dollars. The salesperson tries to get me to buy fancy shoelaces for an extra ten bucks. No thanks.

8. I go home. The shoes seem to be cheaply made. If I want to return them, I have to take them back to the store. That would be a big hassle, so I keep them.

9. I wear them to the gym. My best friend remarks, "Oh yeah, I had a pair of Tenny Shoes once. After two months, they fell apart."

10. Two months after I bought them, the rubber sole separates from the upper part of the shoe. I toss the sneakers in the Goodwill box and vow to never buy another pair.

The sales transaction is a delicate and fragile thing and like a soufflé, can collapse very easily.

In the first scenario, Tenny Shoe delivered on my expectations. They even *exceeded* my expectations. In the second scenario, they fell down. The delivery did not match the image they had built about the store and its products.

Speaking of sneakers, here's a real-life example of a salesperson going the extra mile to exceed my expectations. In 2014 I happened to visit a New Balance store in Baton Rouge, Louisiana. A few days after I had bought a pair of shoes at the store, I received a personal thank-you note from the salesperson. Since my initial visit, I have contacted him twice, and he maintains records of each sale and has my shoe size, and he obviously takes notes because he remembers details about my purchases. I have ordered two more pairs over the phone, which they have shipped to my home in Lafayette, about an hour away. The level of attention has made a huge impression on me, and not only do I remember his service, but I've told several people about it; and since then I've purchased only from him. And, sure enough, he sends a note after every purchase.

Product vs. Service-Based Businesses

Regardless of the type of business—retail, online, service, products, or a combination—all businesses offer one of two things:

- Products—retail, like a lamp or a clock or a flashlight.
- Service—carwash, massage therapy, DNA testing.

Let's first talk about a product-based business.

Product-Based Business

Obviously, the quality of your product should be the highest possible which allows you to meet or exceed your target market's expectations while still ensuring a profitable operation. Moreover, you must deliver the *value* that the price demands. You can sell at whatever price point you want as long as your product delivers commiserate value and there is a market willing to pay for that level of quality. Take laptop computers, for example. In the laptop marketplace, there are Apple MacBooks, and then there is everyone else. As of this writing, the *cheapest* Apple laptop is the basic MacBook Air for $900. Most MacBooks sell for between $1,000 and $3,000.

Meanwhile, you can buy a decent Dell or HP laptop for $300. Does this mean that every consumer will buy Dells or HPs, which are cheaper? No. The question is not which laptop is cheaper, but *which one delivers the most value* at its price point. Most computer manufacturers offer a computer at every price point so that a customer who says, for example, "I have $2,000 to spend on a laptop," can find one at that price. For its part, Apple has chosen not to compete in the $300 laptop market. They don't think they can meet the expectations of the Apple customer at that price and still make a profit.

Let's assume that your product is of the best possible quality and is priced competitively with the competition. Does this mean that it will fly off the shelves? Not necessarily. Remember our transaction with Tenny Shoe? Even if you are in the business of selling a product, a significant part of every transaction with your customer involves the *service* you provide. Whether you like it or not, you're always in the service business.

This becomes even more important when you're in a highly competitive, commoditized business, like selling pizza. Let's face it—there's only so much you can do to a pizza to make it unique. And even if you managed to create a truly new pizza, you couldn't patent it, so anybody could copy and sell it themselves. Therefore, your ability to make a profit will be dependent upon the *customer experience* you provide.

At Front Street, the pizza place I discussed in a previous chapter, the individual items it offered for sale—the pizza, the appetizers, the booze—were not unique. It was the customer experience—the décor, the staff, the service, even the small details, such as the good quality flatware and nice cotton napkins—that created a sense of value. At Front Street, its product is really *customer happiness*, which it just happens to achieve by selling pizza. As long as its delivery system meets or exceeds my friend's expectations, he'll be going back again and again.

Product-Based Business in a New Digital Economy

Remember Borders Books? In 2010 Borders operated 511 book superstores in the United States, as well as 175 stores in the Waldenbooks Specialty Retail segment.

Its end came quickly and brutally. On February 16, 2011, Borders applied for Chapter 11 bankruptcy protection and began liquidating 226 of its stores in the United States. The last remaining stores closed their doors in September of the same year.

What did Borders miss? In a word, the Internet.

Borders stood by and watched as online book sales grew. Borders eventually responded by outsourcing its online bookselling to Amazon. So anytime you visited Borders.com, you were redirected to Amazon.com. While at the time it may have seemed like a rational decision to leverage the Amazon juggernaut, relinquishing control to another company hurt Borders' branding strategies and cut into its customer base.

Borders didn't foresee the rise of ebooks as Amazon and later Barnes & Noble did. It didn't develop its own e-reader to compete with the Kindle or the Nook, and Borders was late to open an online ebook store. And when you walked into a Borders, you barely knew that they sold ebooks for devices, like the Kobo and Cruz. These were external environmental threats that Borders failed to recognize and respond to quickly enough.

If you run a brick and mortar operation, then you too are competing with the Amazons of the world where customers can just go online and their purchase is shipped to their door the next day. Rather than wait for the UPS man to bring it to their doors, you've got to use your benefits and your strategy because your target audience is going to prefer to see and touch it in person, look at your inventory for options, leave with it in a bag or box, and bring it home that day. That's the difference in knowing how your customer wants to be served.

If you're a retailer at a mall and for whatever reason traffic isn't getting to your store, you need to either work with the mall to fix the problem or get ready to move. Whatever interferes with your ability to deliver your product to your customer, whether internal or external, needs to be attacked and fixed pronto.

Giving More Value Costs Less

Treating your customers like royalty doesn't cost you a penny more than treating them like peasants. You can create valuable goodwill by providing exceptional person-to-person service—and you never know who will walk through your door.

A few years ago a restaurant opened near the home of my friend Joe. Actually, new owners had taken over a failed location, but that's nothing unusual; it happens every day in the restaurant business. By coincidence, my friend Joe operates a community blog called "Good Morning Joe." Every day he and his friends post news and photos on the blog, and since he's been doing it for many years, the blog has become very popular. Almost everyone in town reads the blog at least once a day, and they like seeing the photos of local sights and reading local news. "Good Morning Joe" also boosts local businesses—any time a business has a special event, like a ladies' night, the blog is happy to spread the word to its thousands of readers.

Joe was happy that there was a new Italian restaurant in town. He emailed the owner and asked for information about the grand opening, the menu, and special dishes. The owner sent him all sorts of press releases and photos, which Joe posted on the blog. The posts got hundreds of hits, indicating that people had seen the information. Basically, Joe was providing *free marketing and publicity* for the restaurant. To reach the blog's audience with paid advertising would have cost the owner thousands of dollars.

A few days after the grand opening, Joe went to the restaurant to say hello. The owner was behind the counter. You might have expected the owner to greet Joe warmly, offer him a free drink, or perhaps even a complimentary meal. Or, at least, let Joe know that his blog had helped them to reach their customers and establish their name in town. You certainly would have expected Joe to receive a thank you. Instead, he was greeted with a standard greeting and handed a menu.

The clueless owner showed *zero appreciation* for Joe's unpaid efforts. Joe wasn't looking for free food—he's a classy guy—but to not even get a "thank you" was tough to take. Joe didn't stay in the restaurant very long. He left and decided that the blog would no longer promote the restaurant. Why should he? The owner didn't seem to care.

Here's the point of the story: A year later, the restaurant closed its doors. Bankrupt. *Finito.* Joe wasn't surprised. It didn't matter how good the food was—the owner had no clue about good customer service or community relations.

Most small businesses fail. In fact, eight out of ten entrepreneurs who start businesses fail within the first 18 months. It sounds like a dismal ratio, but I think many businesses fail because owners simply don't focus on the right things at the right times. Too often when you look behind the scenes of a failed business, the reasons are painfully clear. Owners are not focused on delivering value. They tolerate poor service. They don't build up a network of raving fans. They insist on trying to sell a product that no one wants, or—perhaps the worst of all—they try to do everything themselves and get burned out. Having spent all their time as mechanics rather than drivers of their businesses they, and their businesses, ran out of gas.

Service-Based Business

The other type of business is a service business—carwash, massage therapy, DNA testing. In a service business, while there may be significant back-room technology or infrastructure, you're typically not *transferring ownership of an item* from the company to the customer. You're providing something *intangible*, often on a person-to-person basis. This may be advice, information, cleaning, medical services, entertainment, financial services—the list is long.

Let's take the example of dry cleaning as a service. Every neighborhood has a dry cleaning establishment. The process itself is fairly ordinary: the customer drops off the garment and comes back two or three days later to pick up the garment, which has been cleaned and pressed. The chances are good that one dry cleaner doesn't get the garment any "cleaner" than another dry cleaner; after all, clean is clean, right? So if your dry cleaning establishment is located in a neighborhood with one or more competitors, how do you differentiate yourself and exceed customer expectations?

There are several ways:

1. Your front-line customer service reps.

Every interaction between a customer and your front-line staff needs to be positive and pleasant. Think about the nature of the business—who *wants* to visit the dry cleaner? Probably nobody. It's a necessary chore—necessary, but still a chore. Therefore, your staff should make this bit of daily drudgery as pleasant and painless as possible.

Remember, this entire book—the whole Mulligan Method—is based on the idea that you, as the owner, need to be able to step away from the day-to-day operation and focus on the Seven Systems that actually drive your business. Among other things, this means that you need front-line people who are properly trained and skilled at working with the public.

You cannot hover over their shoulders as they serve your customers. Before they talk to a single customer, they need to *understand your expectations*, and they need to be motivated to *exceed your expectations*. In this way, the staff works in your business, so you can work on it, driving it farther and faster to success.

2. Delivery time and condition.

If you say the garment will be ready at 10:00 am on Tuesday, you'd better have it ready by 9:00 am, just in case the customer shows up early. The garment needs to be fresh and ready to wear. No excuses. If a problem has arisen—for example, if the fabric is fragile and became damaged—this needs to be explained up front. Never be evasive.

3. Free pickup and delivery.

This is a very attractive service, but it must be regular and reliable. Nothing will infuriate a customer more quickly than to be told, "We apologize that our delivery person is late. Your garment is on the truck. The driver is out on his rounds. We're sorry you're going to miss the gala dinner because we didn't deliver your dress in time . . ."

4. Your cleaning system.

Customers want to feel good about how they spend their money and about the businesses they patronize. For example, as you probably know, "dry cleaning" is not "dry"; it can best be described as "cleaning using chemical solvents instead of water." Some people view these chemicals as unsafe, and today more and more consumers are seeking out and even paying extra for service businesses that reflect their personal values— including "green" dry cleaners. So choosing such a system is a way to differentiate your business from competitors.

These considerations are all part of your delivery system—and can make the difference. So, consider carefully the service you are providing and the concerns of your target market and develop a delivery system designed to address those particular concerns.

Quick Death vs. Slow Death

So far, we have looked at three critical systems: attraction, conversion, and delivery. And, if you think about any business, you'll understand that without one of these three systems, you're out of business. In keeping with the car theme, these are the systems that can cause fatal crashes. For example, if you are suddenly unable to attract leads—you're out of business. If you can attract leads but cannot convert them into paying customers—you're out of business. And, if for some reason you cannot effectively deliver your products or services to the leads that have converted into customers—you will quickly find yourself out of business.

The same is true with the next four of the seven systems. However, if you don't give these systems the proper focus the death of your business may be prolonged, but death will still occur. As you continue reading, you'll see how the following four systems are each connected to the other systems. And, you'll see how vital they are to your Business Mulligan.

As we look at the next four systems, we'll start with your company's culture. As I said above, your culture is found in each system of your business—down to the part and component part. By investing the time to identify your company's values, purpose, and mission statement, you really begin to experience the positive energy your Mulligan can bring to your business. By empowering your team with the overall goals of your company, you will find freedom to work on your business.

Key Concepts

- Exceeding expectations increases value for the customer. Provide the fresh lemon wedge.
- Delivering value turns satisfied customers into referral sources.
- Delivering value provides opportunities for upsells and repeat business from a happy customer.

Action Plan

Go to www.businessmulligan.com/snapshot and list all products or services you currently deliver to your customers.

1. How does the customer perceive your business? Be honest. What messages are you sending that set up the customer's expectations? Can you meet these expectations?

2. Is your business primarily a product-based business, or do you provide a service?

3. If it's a product, is it easy to buy? How is it delivered? Is it fully guaranteed? Do you know where your product fits in comparison to those of your competitors?

4. If it's a service business, have you analyzed the customer transaction from beginning to end? Have you trained your people to be unfailingly polite and helpful? Does your staff respond quickly and cheerfully to customer complaints?

5. Repeat customers are the lifeblood of any business. Do you have a rewards program to encourage customers to stay with you? When customers come into your store or office, or log onto your website, do you greet them by name? What steps do you take to ensure your business is seen as a vital part of your community?

6. How often do you write thank-you notes to your customers?

SEVEN

System 4: Culture

Why?

Why do we do what we do?

If you have been a little slow on the uptake when it comes to "culture," I get it. I used to think that business was always about marketing, sales, and customer service. I figured that if we could get and keep customers, we were doing pretty well. It was not until I read an article about creating a code of honor for your employees to operate by that I decided to try what I considered "touchy feely stuff." And this "touchy feely stuff" allowed our team to manage each other, freeing me up to work on my business and be away from it too.

The DNA Way

Early on in my business, things were going well, but since the DNA industry was experiencing so much change due to technological advances, all the changes began to wear on our team. I invited the entire team to a retreat with the sole goal of creating our code of honor. I began discussing why I thought we needed a code to operate by and asked everyone to think about their personal values as well as what they think is important at work. I told everyone that there was no perfect list. Instead, I wanted to end up with a list that we could use to basically police ourselves with, something that everyone had a hand in creating, so they each had an invested interest in it.

We spent two days coming up with a set of statements that ultimately became our guiding principles. We called them "The DNA Way." Below is the list of statements that not only helped us guide our actions but also guided our decisions. Best of all, anyone could respectfully call anyone out when they didn't operate—The DNA Way.

1. *Team dedication and commitment*
2. *Excellence in customer experience*
3. *Growth through open communication*
4. *Doing what we say we will do*
5. *Selling = seize the opportunity*
6. *Earn respect—give respect to self, team, and client*
7. *Culture that appreciates family*
8. *Success through education*
9. *Setting goals collectively*
10. *Perpetual improvement*

As you can see, these statements weren't crystal clear to someone who wasn't on our team. But, for everyone who participated in the creation of the code, we knew exactly what they meant.

Once we got those in place and I witnessed the positive effects that code creation process had on each member of our team, we began addressing each code and implementing it into our company's culture.

What Is Culture?

The culture of any business is comprised of its philosophical ideals, moral values, and priorities which govern the company's policies and practices. It impacts how the company treats its employees, its customers and fundamentally determines how the business will operate. Understanding the significance of your company's culture will make you a better leader and make your business better.

Culture illustrates the accepted norms, values, and traditional behavior of a group. It can evolve over time. Culture influences management, decisions, and all business functions from accounting to production. A business culture encompasses an organization's values, visions, working style, beliefs, and habits.

Because it encompasses tradition and risk, a strong culture can help get a company through the inevitable difficult times that can strike at any stage of business. There are times when you or your team may feel like packing it in or passing over the little things that make a big difference. During these times, knowing your *why* is critical. It will be the motivation you need, the encouragement you need, and the hope you need when you don't feel like doing it.

Motivation comes from many different sources. Some of your team might be internally motivated. They are principle-driven and have a strong work ethic. They will give their all because that's what they do. Some need verbal encouragement, privately or publicly, while others need financial incentives.

Successful business owners find ways to motivate everyone on their team. Really successful businesses unify all of those sources of motivation by giving people a *why*, a reason for doing what they do. A reason that goes beyond employees' individual goals, company goals, work ethic, and individuals' responsiveness to external motivators, and this *why* also ignites their passion.

With a clear and powerful *why*, when times are tough or the work is difficult, employees can say, "But if I don't do this, then _____ will happen." Or "_____ are counting on us to do this." Or "When we do _____, we are making a difference in people's lives." Or "We are giving people _____, and that's important because_____."

You Are the Leader

Culture is a top-down phenomenon. While extremely large businesses can have influential subcultures, in my experience in working with many businesses, I've discovered that those that have exciting, positive, and healthy *cultures* have excited, passionate, positive, and healthy *leaders*.

This means that before your team can tap into its deeper motivation, you must tap into yours. Ralph Waldo Emerson noted, "Nothing great has ever been accomplished in human history without enthusiasm." If you want your people to be enthusiastic, passionate, purpose-filled, excited, and positive, you must model that for them.

So, what is your *why*?

This sounds like such a simple question, but once you give it some thought, you will realize how difficult it is. As tempted as you may be to skip this analysis, don't. This is critical. And remember it's not the easy questions that make great businesses and leaders; it's the difficult questions that have the power to pull us from where we are to where we want to be.

Here are two questions:

1. *Why* did you get started in this business?
2. *Why* are you in this business right now?

For many, these questions result in two totally different answers. Often, the reason we start something isn't the reason we continue doing it. This is true not only in your business but in every area of your life. For some, as we mentioned earlier, you started a business because you wanted freedom and you wanted to be your own boss. And if you're still reading this book, by this point, it's likely you've realized you're no longer your own boss. Your customers and team are your bosses. They set your schedule, not you.

Chances are you've not had much freedom in a while, so why are you still in business? Why do you still get up and go to work in the morning? These answers are likely more practical: to pay the bills, make ends meet, because your employees and customers are counting on you to show up. These are good reasons.

But what if there is or could be a deeper reason?

Purpose

Viktor Frankl, an Austrian psychiatrist and survivor of Auschwitz concentration camp, once noted, "Man can deal with any *how*, provided he possesses a strong enough *why*." What powerful words from someone who found a way to survive one of the most difficult experiences imaginable.

His message is essentially this: if you know why you're doing something and if that *why* is strong enough, that purpose will provide sufficient motivation to ensure the means – the how – is satisfied. It might not be easy or simple, but it will be doable. If it's not, then the *why* needs some work.

What if you got out of bed in the morning because you were excited to get to work on something you were passionate about?

What if you showed up at work energized, excited, passionate, and hopeful because you knew that the work you and your team were doing was important to the lives of other people?

Let's look at it from a different perspective—the end of life perspective. There has been lots of research done with people who are dying. It shows that when people are dying, when they know they're nearing the end of their lives, they all ask three basic questions:

- Did I really live my life?
- Did I really love the people in my life?
- Did I do something that mattered?

These are not questions we ask in our daily grind. Because these questions are so deep and powerful, we often don't feel like we have the time to answer or ponder them. But I'm inviting you to do that now. If you had to account for the time you've spent on this earth and answer these three questions today, what would the answers be?

- Did I live?
- Did I really live my life?
- Did I get out of my comfort zone to create new experiences?
- Did I reach my potential?
- Did I go after my dreams?
- Did I allow fear or possibility to control my life?
- Did I love?
- Did I spend time getting to know those who are important to me?
- Did I risk being vulnerable and share myself with those who are important to me?
- Did I give of myself to my family and friends?
- Did the people in my life feel like they really knew me and I knew them?
- Did I matter?
- Did I do something important and significant with my time on this earth?
- Did I make a contribution to the world, to other people in the world?
- Did I risk anything in order to make the lives of other people better?

This is a powerful inventory. But these are questions you can ask not only yourself but your team as well. Apply these questions to your business. Is your business alive? Can people look at your business and see what or whom you love? Do you love your customers? Does what you do matter? Is your motivation, your purpose, and your goal to help your community be a better place with your products or services?

Once you get clear on why your business truly matters, the answers can generate a passion that is contagious. The love you have for your customers becomes apparent. The reasons your company exists shine brightly for all to see. Your team becomes united behind a cause and that liberates you, the owner, because you know that each one of your employees loves your customers and operates with a higher level of pride and purpose.

Mission

Every company needs a mission. At DNA Services of America, our mission was helping people discover the truth through DNA testing. Very simple, but it was all about helping, discovering, and truth— universal ideas people can buy into.

One of the overarching missions of my life is to serve and give my best self to create the best life that God can give me and to give my very best self to others. That gets me up every morning.

When you stop and think about why you were put on this earth and for what purpose, you can make a difference. If your business doesn't have a mission, then you're just in business; you're just operating. Similar to a life where you just exist and you're not living, you don't want your business to just exist; you want it to thrive. Until you clarify and state your mission, you can't operate with intention.

Your mission needs to be stated in writing. Your mission statement is not the same as your company's slogan or tag line, which generally serves as a marketing tool designed to quickly focus the consumer's attention. The mission statement is also not the same as your vision statement, which defines where you want your company to go. And while you may include the mission statement in your business plan, it's not a substitute for the plan itself.

It's important to remember that a mission statement is not carved in stone. As your company evolves over time, your mission and intent may also change. If you keep it visible, your mission statement will keep your company on track, but you can't let it become stale or obsolete, so revisit it every few years to adjust it if necessary. When your mission motivates you, it will motivate your team. A motivated team is an empowered team. An empowered team gives you freedom. It becomes a driving force behind your Business Mulligan.

What does a mission statement include? A good mission statement answers several key questions about your business:

• What are the opportunities or needs that the company addresses?

• What is the business of the organization? How are these needs being addressed?

• What level of service is provided?

• What principles or beliefs guide the organization?

The best way to develop your mission statement is to hold open meetings with the stakeholders of your business, including your employees and investors. Ask them what they see as your business's biggest strengths and weaknesses. It's important to see how a variety of people view your company so that you have more than one perspective. Take your time when writing the statement; it may take more than a few drafts, with each successive draft being circulated for review and comment.

A good place to start is by defining your company's core values. You can also incorporate into your mission statement your company's story. Start with a concise story that describes what you're trying to accomplish.

The value of a mission statement is felt when all stakeholders see it, can understand it, and use it as an internal business compass for when they make their day-to-day decisions. Consequently, mission statements need to be written using words and sentences that regular people use and understand. If it's written in dense industry jargon, it won't have any impact.

Once the mission statement is complete, it should be displayed with pride inside and outside the business. Post the mission statement in the office, print it on company materials, and be prepared to share it with potential customers.

Examples of Mission Statements

Here are a few mission statements from well-known companies. As you can see, mission statements can be short or long. Some even incorporate bullet points and subparagraphs.

- Amazon—*To be the most customer-centric company in the world, where people can find and discover anything they want to buy online.*
- Starbucks—*To inspire and nurture the human spirit—one person, one cup, and one neighborhood at a time.*
- Uber—*Transportation as reliable as running water, everywhere, for everyone.*

Vision

Your mission empowers your team by helping them understand why you're in business. A vision is the image of what your business aspires to be at some point in the future. A vision helps your team see what it can become. When they can see it, they can believe it's possible and likely will work harder to achieve it.

A vision statement should communicate your long-term business goals and should reflect your view of the world and your business's place in it. It captures, in writing, the essence of where the business is going and can inspire you and your staff to reach your goals.

It should also answer the fundamental question, "Where are we going?" In contrast, the practical aspect of "What do we want to accomplish?" is usually dealt with in a mission statement or a business plan.

Having a vision will give your business a clear focus and can help the company head in the right direction.

Just like your mission, the best way to make your vision real to everyone is to write it. To write an effective vision statement you should consider what your business does and imagine what your business would look like if it became the best possible version of itself.

As with the mission statement, getting stakeholder input is necessary—both to get a wide range of viewpoints and to foster stakeholder buy-in once the vision statement is adopted. A good first step in developing a vision statement is to invite your key staff to a business vision workshop. By brainstorming and sharing ideas, you can answer fundamental questions about the direction of your business, which will make it much easier to write your vision statement. After you've held your vision workshop—or a series of them—and have come up with a portfolio of ideas, you're ready to write a draft vision statement. Make sure your vision statement:

- is short and says a lot in a few words,
- is clear and written in plain English, with no industry jargon,
- doesn't use numeric measures of success,
- is passionate, powerful, and memorable,
- describes the ideal state for your business,
- helps people visualize a clear picture of what the best version of the company looks like,
- and, is realistic in terms of your resources, capabilities, and growth potential.

As you formulate your company's vision, ask, "What's possible?" Great leaders and great businesses regularly ask this question. Many businesses systematize this question in order to make sure not only the organization is asking it, but that each department, each team, and each individual are always asking that powerful question: what is possible here?

Sure, reality will often demand you move, shift and execute without fully realizing what could be possible. But if the culture of the business isn't one of possibility, then complacency, which is a cancer in any business, will slowly seep in, and the life, energy, and enthusiasm of your people will die. The reach and success of your business will begin dying with them.

We are hardwired to dream. But, when we were younger, most of us were criticized for being dreamers. "Your head's in the clouds; you need to come back to earth." "Sure that's a fine major in college, but you're not going to make any money doing that!"

Research shows that from time we're born, we've heard twenty no's for each yes.

- Q: Can I do that . . . ?
- A: *No.*
- Q: What would it be like if . . . ?
- A: *Eh . . . probably not going to happen.*

We hear that often enough, and we begin to believe it. And once we internalize it, we stop asking:

- What's possible?
- What am I capable of?
- What are we capable of doing?
- How far can we go?
- How good can we be?

Leaders ask possibility questions of themselves, others, and the organization, and then use every resource they can to paint a clear picture of what's possible in the future. In doing this they ignite passion, creativity, and enthusiasm. If you were to look inside any successful business, you'd find a visionary leader who envisioned a compelling future and was very good at getting people to see his or her picture and believe it was possible. That's what great leaders do.

But they start with themselves. They are regularly asking themselves:

- What's possible for me as a leader?
- What could I become?
- What am I capable of?

They brainstorm, they visualize, they talk, they continually evaluate and reassess what a better future would look like and the ways to achieve it, because they know—if you're not growing, you're dying.

Examples of Vision Statements

While large companies often have a grand vision statement that presents global goals, even a small business can benefit from having a concise vision statement. Below are some examples of vision statements from four well-known companies:

- Alcoa—*At Alcoa, our vision is to be the best company in the world—in the eyes of our customers, shareholders, communities, and people. We expect and demand the best we have to offer by always keeping Alcoa's values top of mind.*
- GM—*GM's vision is to be the world leader in transportation products and related services. We will earn our customers' enthusiasm through continuous improvement driven by the integrity, teamwork, and innovation of GM people.*
- Sears—*To be the preferred and most trusted resource for the products and services that enhance home and family life.*
- Tyco—*We will increase the value of our company and our global portfolio of diversified brands by exceeding customers' expectations and achieving market leadership and operating excellence in every segment of our company.*

Choosing Your Employees

Your employees can make or break your business.

When you move from a one- or two-person operation and begin hiring employees, everything changes. The vision you hold for your business needs to become the vision of *every* person on your team. By communicating your shared vision with your teammates, you develop a healthy culture of people who free you up from working under the hood of the business to being behind the wheel and driving the business like you should. When you fail to communicate your vision, your culture becomes dysfunctional and weak, which keeps you trapped.

I've talked to business owners who confide, "If it weren't for employees, I'd love my business." All business owners recognize the challenge of finding and retaining the right employees. However, the critical need to do so is fundamental to the success of your business. So selecting people who are capable of grasping the vision and working hard to achieve it is key.

We often hire too quickly and fire too slowly because we have not created a culture that attracts the right people who will embrace our culture. Attracting the wrong people makes your business vulnerable to negativity and employee dissatisfaction.

Defining the reason your company exists and understanding it is critical to your success. When you don't have buy-in from your team, your business is threatened. The point of hiring and firing with intention based upon the purpose of the business is critical. Attracting the right employees and customers comes from your purpose for being in business.

Too often we hire and fire for a purpose, but not on purpose. What I mean is that we often hire because we need to fill a position and we fire because someone makes a mistake or we just need to reduce payroll. When a clerk or receptionist is needed, we place an ad, interview, and hire the best candidate as quickly as we can. How likely is it that that person is going to work out? My experience is about 50/50.

> *Too often we hire and fire for a purpose, but not on purpose.*

During an interview, people will say *anything* to get the job. I don't want to sound jaded about people like the business owners I described earlier, but that's the experience you will likely have if you just fill positions.

If you take the time to identify your business's purpose, vision, and mission, and you list and live your company values, you'll be able to hire and fire with intention. Hire the next employee on purpose because they embody your company's values, because they have determined that their life has a purpose and it is in harmony with the purpose of your company. And fire those who cannot work within those core principles. Be more intentional about whom you share this business with, and you'll see an increase in the number of employees who stay with you year after year. These people, because of their acquired experience and knowledge, can take the wheel and drive when you need a break.

Training

Each of your Seven Systems needs clear and flexible procedures, which allow you to thoroughly train and empower your team. A well-trained, empowered team is what frees you up to work on your business—to take your Business Mulligan. Training is a critical piece of that goal. Ongoing training of your team is a must.

As you develop your values, you can share them. One of mine is "Perpetual improvement". You have to develop the mindset that training is never-ending and continuous improvement is the ultimate goal. There will be times when you ask the question, "Where am I needed most right now?" and the answer is on the eighth day of a 14-day vacation. Of course, you are the driver of your business, but sometimes you need other people to take the wheel, and they have to know and embrace your vision so they can drive the business in a way consistent with its purpose and to move it toward its vision.

Once you have identified an employee who is complacent and you have accepted that they cannot improve, it should be clear that they no longer fit within your company structure. Although it requires more of an effort to find the right people to join your team and to keep them striving for improvement, that effort will be well spent. It will translate into the ability to get away from your business and recharge, the importance of which cannot be overstated. It will also translate into a decrease of anxiety and worry regarding the daily operations of your company. The emotional drain which often deprives you of both the time and the energy to direct your attention where it is most needed in order to grow it.

Leadership Development

Your most senior people are the ones who are going to take on the responsibility of running your company day to day while you work on the business to improve or expand it. They are the ones who are in the business, so you can work on the business. Ensuring that they can handle responsibility as well as represent you and your company is critical. You're most likely the face of your company, but your leaders represent you when you're not there. They can support or undermine the mission, and if not, they are not adequately developed.

Reading current leadership books, taking developmental courses on management, and studying team building can help you to develop your leaders. You should work to help them improve professionally in their fields of expertise, but also as individuals. Ideally, they should improve both personally and professionally. As your employees grow personally, they will also grow professionally. The value you help add to them personally will be felt throughout each system of your business. For example, by encouraging them to volunteer and mentor a younger associate or team member, you will see their leadership skills grow while improving the performance of another team member.

The first three of the seven systems were more directly focused on your customer. As you've seen, the culture system is more directly focused on your company. The same is true of the next three systems, each of which affect your entire company and each of the other systems and their parts, ultimately benefitting your customer and the health of your entire company.

Now that you're working on developing a healthy culture of empowered and motivated team members and you understand *why* you're in business, you can identify, document, and even implement systems that help your team members understand *how* to actually do business. This is what we'll be addressing in the next chapter.

Key Concepts

- Your purpose gives your team motivation.
- Your mission gives your team direction.
- Your vision gives your team a destination.
- Your values keep you and your team headed in the right direction to reach your destination.
- Your mission, vision, purpose, and values drive everything in your business: whom you hire, whom you fire, the customers you attract, and the ones you don't.
- Finding employees who embrace your purpose, mission and vision will free you to manage your business and your life more effectively.

Action Plan

Go to www.businessmulligan.com/snapshot to identify which parts of culture are in place and which are missing in order to create your company's culture.

- If your company doesn't have a mission statement, write one.
- If you have one, make sure it's visible and reviewed regularly.
- A vision statement is optional, but useful.
- Think about your company culture and employees. Do you effectively communicate the company culture to new hires? Do

you work with existing employees who don't seem to get it? And, as a last resort, are you willing to terminate someone who insists upon "doing it their own way" despite your continued efforts to bring them onto the team?

EIGHT

System 5: Systems

How?

How do we operate profitably?

A Shock to My System

My first real memory of effective systems occurred in the late evening of March 20, 1988. Yes, it made quite an impression on me. I arrived in San Diego, CA around 7:30pm and was previously instructed to meet my ride downstairs, at the south side of the airport, at 8:45pm. While I was waiting, I had a great conversation with a guy from Ohio. His hair was so long in the back that it touched his beltline. As we continued to wait more passengers showed up and we had a great time meeting each other and finding out where everyone was from.

A bus pulled up at exactly 8:45pm and a very large, very loud, very angry sailor jumped out. He captured our attention immediately and quickly explained to us what was about to happen. He held a clipboard and called out our names. One-by-one we stepped onto the bus and sat down in the seats, filling up the back of the bus first and working our way to the front, exactly as he had instructed.

The bus pulled off as soon as the last recruit sat down and the instructions continued until we arrived at our home for the next several weeks. We got out and were instructed to line up. You would think there would be some confusion any time you gather a group of young men, but this was a well-oiled machine. There were yellow footprints painted on the concrete, so there was no confusion where each of us should stand. We were then told that we were going to call home to inform our parents or loved ones that we had arrived safely. We were led to a bank of about ten phones, in line and affixed to the wall. We were instructed to read the written statement that was posted on the wall, above the phone. It went something like this:

"I have arrived safely in San Diego.

Please do not send any food or bulky items.

I will contact you in seven to ten days via postcard with my new mailing address.

Thank you for your support.

Goodbye for now."

For the next 10 weeks we didn't waste a second. And, we quickly learned that this is how our days were going to go. The next morning we found ourselves in an orderly line to get haircuts. I no longer recognized my longhaired buddy or any of the other guys who claimed to be so tough and that nobody could tell them what to do. Little did they know that every minute of every day for the next ten weeks was built into a detailed system. I'm sure the drill instructors could tell them exactly what they would be doing, but that would have spoiled all the fun.

The first four of the seven systems we've covered—attraction, conversion, delivery, and culture—focus on what you do to make your business a success. You might say they relate to what happens on a daily basis within the four walls of your store or office.

In this system—which is simply called "systems"—we'll identify the framework and tools that provide the structure for your daily activities. The systems system is about how you and your team do business. Ultimately, by identifying, documenting, and implementing systems in your business, you'll be free to stop working in your business and able to work on it.

For example, your place of business—store, factory, or office—must be laid out and designed in such a way as to maximize efficiency. If the building is too complex or people can't work easily within it, then your business will suffer. Inefficiency and wasted time will sap productivity and eat away at your margins, thus drawing you out of the driver's seat and back under the hood.

The same holds true for your car. Under the hood of your car are groups of parts linked together to form systems. They include the drivetrain, braking system, exhaust system, electrical system, climate-control system, steering, entertainment—the list is long. Each of these systems must be elegantly designed, efficient, and work seamlessly together. And if one of them is subpar, it will affect the performance of the car itself, again putting you back under the hood, working in your business and not on it.

Likewise, in your business the systems that you use—which include software applications that interface with physical systems like cash registers, telephones, inventory control devices, HVAC systems, and security systems—must be independently efficient while working seamlessly together.

The goal of all of these systems is to increase productivity, lower operating costs, shorten response times, reduce errors, increase customer satisfaction, and—perhaps best of all—allow you, the owner, to sleep peacefully at night knowing your business is humming along on its own, so all you have to do is drive it.

If you use multiple operations systems that are not unified, you may be making your job harder than it has to be. For example, if you're using ConstantContact for your email marketing, LeadPages for building landing pages, and a separate customer relationship management (CRM) program to store your contacts, it gets overwhelming because you have multiple places where you have the same information. Because you can't tie them together, it creates an organizational mess where a lot of things fall through the cracks.

When and if you can find tools that are all-in-one or interface easily, using them in your overall system can save you time, energy and hours of frustration.

It's important to document your systems, so other people can easily operate them in your absence, and if they are well documented, others can take those documents and ensure they are being implemented correctly, empowering your employees to work in your business and systems, while you work on it.

Operations and Systems Manual

Every business needs an operations manual—a clear guide to the various systems that anyone could follow. It may take time to develop, but it will be worth it. You should go to the trouble of writing down your procedures for several very good reasons.

Reason 1—It creates measurable standards.

When it comes to products and customer service, customers seek consistency, not random and inconsistent acts of super service. If you provide a customer with one experience and your employees give that same customer another experience, in the eyes of that customer the quality of the business will be diminished. A written plan will make sure everyone knows what expectations you have set for your business and employees.

As an extreme example, a big chain like McDonald's uses highly detailed and specific systems for every aspect of restaurant operations.

In fact, they call it the "McDonald's System." The franchisee contract that McDonald's uses is fifteen pages long and spells out very clearly what the franchisee needs to do in order to ensure that the customer who, for example, patronizes McDonald's #367 in Chicago will have the same customer experience as when he or she patronizes McDonald's #953 in San Diego. The agreement states, in part:

"Manuals: McDonald's shall provide Franchisee with the business manuals prepared for use by franchisees of McDonald's restaurants similar to the Restaurant. The business manuals contain detailed information including: (a) required operations procedures; (b) methods of inventory control; (c) bookkeeping and accounting procedures; (d) business practices and policies; and (e) other management and advertising policies.

Franchisee agrees to promptly adopt and use exclusively the formulas, methods, and policies contained in the business manuals, now and as they may be modified from time to time . . . .

Compliance with entire system: Franchisee acknowledges that every component of the McDonald's System is important to McDonald's and to the operation of the Restaurant as a McDonald's Restaurant, including a designated menu of food and beverage products; uniformity of food specifications, preparation methods, quality, and appearance; and uniformity of facilities and service.

McDonald's shall have the right to inspect the Restaurant at all reasonable times to ensure that Franchisee's operation thereof is in compliance with the standards and policies of the McDonald's System.

Franchisee shall comply with the entire McDonald's System, including, but not limited to, the following:

I (a) Operate the Restaurant in a clean, wholesome manner in compliance with prescribed standards of Quality, Service, and Cleanliness; comply with all business policies, practices, and procedures imposed by McDonald's; serve at the Restaurant only those food and beverage products now or hereafter designated by McDonald's; and maintain the building, fixtures, equipment, signage, decor, and parking area in a good, clean, wholesome condition and repair, and well lighted and in compliance with designated standards as may be prescribed from time to time by McDonald's."

While it's not necessary that you publish your operations manual with the same detail as McDonald's, the rationale is identical: a well-written manual empowers your employees to take more responsibility for the day-to-day operation of your business, freeing you from putting out fires and making endless small decisions that eat up your time. It helps ensure that your customers have a consistent experience. And if the day should come that you want to open another store or a branch office, you've got the manual in hand for getting it up and running quickly. A well-written manual then is another necessary component for putting you in the driver's seat of your business.

Reason 2—It results in better-trained employees.

If you're like most small business owners, you probably walk new employees through every step personally, explaining what needs to be done and what you expect from them. Do you do the same exact thing for every employee that you hire? Probably not. What will happen if your manager needs to start training new hires? Will the training be the same? A written training plan will ensure that all new hires are given the same information to help create consistency among all of your employees. It will also allow you to delegate some training responsibilities to other employees without diminishing the impact of that training.

It can be something very simple. Let's say you walk into the Tenny Shoe store, and within ten seconds a customer service employee says, "Hi there. How may I help you?" This sets your standard of expectation for Tenny Shoe stores. A month later you visit another Tenny Shoe store. You walk in and see an employee sitting behind the counter. She doesn't look up. In fact, she seems intent upon ignoring you. This is mildly irritating. Once she gets around to talking to you, her initial behavior may not be a deal breaker, but it can leave a bad taste in your mouth because it was not consistent with your previous experience at the Tenny Shoe store. By clearly articulating your expectations of specific tasks required from each employee you empower them to meet those expectations.

Reason 3—It makes your business more valuable.

Do you have an exit strategy? One day, for various reasons, you may want to sell your business. In the eyes of a prospective buyer, saying, "This is the way we always do things," is much less valuable than saying, "Here is the way we operate our business." Nobody is going to want to buy the ideas in your head; they want tangible proof that your business can function autonomously without the boss running around telling everyone what to do. An operations manual is proof that you have a real business, something that can run with or without the owner present.

This process of looking at your business in parts can help you see how your business is comprised of systems, each needing to be documented. As you go through the process of identifying the different parts, you need supporting documentation, and it needs to be organized according to your snapshot. It needs to be organized in systems, parts, and component parts similar to chapters, sections, and paragraphs of a book. But each part must have a systems manual if you are going to be freed up and not be the one who is always doing it. You can outsource, or even insource, this process.

Your portfolio of systems needs to be broken down into systems developed for operational efficiency. The documentation of the systems needs to be put together like a book. For example, in a service business, like a dentist's office, a system for setting appointments provides greater operational efficiency. It is how you track appointments. When someone makes an appointment, you need to make sure they show up, they're billed, they pay you, a follow-up appointment is set, and that you are available to communicate with them between those appointments. You develop a plan for that particular person. The step-by-step process is a critical component of operating a successful and profitable business because it minimizes recurring "fires."

If you're always recovering from mistakes and putting out fires, you'll never find the time to focus on the big picture of your business. Many of those fires can be avoided if you have a system in place. The more complex your business becomes, the more opportunity there will be for fires that need to be put out. This in turn will put you in the position of the mechanic, always working on small-picture issues, rather than being the driver who moves your business to success by considering the big-picture issues and strategies.

Workflow Automation

Automation allows you to do more with less. Full disclosure here: I am an Infusionsoft Certified Partner. My goal with this book is not to sell you the software or convince you that it is right for your business or required to operate. There are other good options. However, my intention is to illustrate how marketing and workflow automation help make operations more efficient, which creates processes that are far less expensive than paying multiple people to do the same tasks. This creates freedom for individual team members to be more productive, which results in your having more freedom to work on your business and not in it.

You can automate your email marketing, for instance. Instead of paying someone thousands of dollars per month, what if you purchase a software subscription that costs around $200 a month? That's a low salary! This saves you time, money, and confusion. Things don't fall through the cracks any longer, and your customer relationship management (CRM), shopping cart, website, and contact forms are all connected. Because they're all-in-one, you reduce the amount of mistakes and potential mistakes. It's more efficient because you're not jumping from system to system to take a person from potential customer, to a lead, to a customer, to a sale, and then to a repeat customer.

For instance, when I began using Infusionsoft small business software, my life and business changed overnight. We increased our sales. Like many other small business software packages, Infusionsoft offers a suite of capabilities that includes

- CRM
- email follow-up
- marketing automation
- online selling
- sales automation
- systems integration.

The point is that if you haven't investigated small business software recently—and by that, I mean in the past few months—you'll be amazed at what you can get that will help you systematize your business, automate what should be automated, keep tabs on the work of your employees, make quick adjustments as conditions change, and be alerted to potential trouble spots.

It is this type of thinking, planning, and structure that is the foundation of *Business Mulligan*. You'll be able to enjoy a round of golf on the weekend without worrying about your business falling apart.

Marketing Automation

It's important to be top of mind when the customer is ready to buy.

With today's technology, if you have a person's name and contact information, including their mobile phone number, email address, and home address, then you can use a multimedia marketing approach. You can automate marketing to those contacts by creating sequences that deliver email and direct mail, as well as text messages, automatically on your behalf. You can customize those messages to particular products and services that you offer. Those messages then can come from your email address or your phone number, so when the time is right to buy, they'll contact you directly. Today's tools allow you to appear like you are focused on each person as a customer rather than sending out generic material, all without investing the time required to have a member of your team give that person such individualized attention.

Please remember that marketing automation should be handled with *extreme care*. In a culture where human, person-to-person contact is the most valuable, the last thing you want is for your customer or prospect to feel as though they're being barraged with waves of spam in their inboxes.

Determining when your business is ready to invest in automating marketing is key. Many owners invest in marketing automation programs before they have a solid foundation that can make advanced lead-nurturing campaigns grow. You can't have the ingredients you need for effective marketing automation until you have a steady flow of organic, qualified leads coming through the sales pipeline. Too many marketers without inbound lead generation strategies spend their time trying to squeeze sales from the few leads they have while their competition is going after the huge expanse of the market that's still out there. Have you already identified your avatar? Have you obtained contact information on a significant number of contacts who fall within your target market? Only then are you ready for marketing automation. Otherwise, automated marketing directed to people who have no realistic probability of being converted will not be effective.

Understanding that a large database of leads is required for marketing automation to have any effect on their bottom line, many marketers make a risky investment: they buy lists of contacts to input into their marketing automation system. The risks of list buying are numerous, but most importantly this spam-intensive tactic produces an incredibly low return on investment. Along with the cost of buying these lists, sending unsolicited emails to people who have never requested any information from you leads to low engagement and hurts your IP address reputation, lowering your email deliverability rates.

Marketing automation does not mean, "set it and forget it." When done correctly, effective marketing automation takes time, effort, and resources to implement and maintain for revenue growth. But, this time and effort are much less than what you're currently doing on your own.

Simplify

Human beings naturally complicate things, and our businesses are no exceptions.

We get into business, and as the business changes, we develop systems on the fly, and we end up with workarounds. We need a system for developing systems. Without it we're just putting Band-Aids™ on problems and not treating the causes of the problems. Ultimately we'll end up with systems that are disjointed and workarounds for workarounds.

When systems are disconnected and don't talk to each other, when tools are run by one person and no one else knows how to work them and if you have separate systems for every function, then you hold yourself hostage to employees and disjointed systems. When and where you can plug in an all-in-one, you need to do it—and simplify.

Depending on your business, you may need website development, contact forms, lead magnets, opt-in forms, and much more; and if those are not tied to your contact management system, you have to manually enter the contact's name, which is a waste of time, and it could potentially fall through the cracks. You're taking an email from them, and you're manually emailing them to stay in contact with them. You're manually putting in a tickler system or file system to call them back when that can all be automated through an automated sequence. And then once you convert them into a sale, depending on your service or product, you can automate the delivery of that; for example, if it's a digital product, you can send it through email, and if it's a fulfillment product, you can automate the process even if it involves human beings because they'll get a fulfillment list and complete the orders or deliver them as per your company's business protocol. The appointment can be set automatically, where clients go onto your website or your scheduling system and set an appointment, you can be notified through automation, and you both show up for the appointment. No work is involved for you.

Earlier, we talked about the importance of keeping things kindergarten simple. We have to be intentional about keeping things simple because businesses naturally become more complex than necessary. This unnecessary complexity creates confusion and chaos, which ultimately decrease productivity and profits.

Fixing Follow-up Failure

Follow-up failure is one of the most critical mistakes that a small business owner can make. Most people first come to you as leads, and there's a timeframe when they want to buy the product. They may not be ready to buy it at the moment they contact you. So staying in contact with them until they are ready is critical.

Upsells, cross-sells after the sale, and other chores can be automated, and appointment reminders can be sent to you so that nothing falls through the cracks and so that you can follow up.

Follow-up is important because people buy when they're ready to buy. Earlier in the book I discussed the prospect's buying temperature, as represented on a scale from 1 to 10. People who walk into a car lot are often at a 2 or a 3, and they're just shopping around. Some car salesmen think they need to make a sale to every person who visits the showroom. But you can't expect to move a prospect more than 1 to 2 degrees per contact. That's the reason follow-up is so critical.

As the salesperson, you want to reconnect with the potential buyer. You may not increase their buying temperature, but at a minimum you'll be top of mind when they do get to a 10. If the only people you focus on are the ones who walk onto the lot, you'll never have enough people who happen to walk onto the lot at a 10. No salesperson in the world is going to move them from a 2 to a 10 in the same day. A good salesperson can move them from an 8 to a 10, but not all the way up the ladder from cold to hot.

Prospects all have a certain need and timetable, and there are a lot of variables that go into understanding when your prospect is ready to buy; and without automated procedures that assist you, even if it's only set up to remind you to call, the work becomes more labor-intensive. When you can quickly glance at the calendar and see the day's list of prospects that need a personal touch, that's a victory. You follow up when you said you'd follow up, and you're keeping a promise. That's where the efficiencies occur. They occur when you do what you've said you're going to do and you don't let things fall through the cracks; by keeping your word, you build confidence and credibility in your company. At the same time, you continue the conversation with warm leads, monitoring them as their temperature increases and being there for them when they need you. Well-timed, properly drafted follow-up emails, texts or calls keep you top of mind for the customer, so when they approach a level of 10 and it's time for them to buy, they call you and no one else. So many businesses don't understand the importance of being present and top of mind when the customer is ready to buy. That's why they'll do anything to make the sale. Such high-pressured sale and then the buyers have buyers' remorse and will talk bad about them.

Here's a classic example of being top of mind: if you watch TV, you've seen the endless flood of advertisements for auto insurance. The big companies—Progressive, GEICO, Allstate, State Farm, Farmers, Amica— produce a never-ending stream of TV ads that feature entertaining characters, like Progressive's white-uniformed gal named Flo or the talking GEICO gecko. You may ask, "Why on earth do these companies think they need to be constantly in my face? It seems like I see one of these ads every five minutes!" The answer is very simple: they know that at some time during the year, you'll renew your auto insurance or get a new policy. The problem is—*they have no idea when this is going to happen*. Your buying temperature could suddenly go from a 5 to a 10, and you'll want to buy auto insurance in the morning, the afternoon, or the middle of the night, winter, spring, summer, or fall—it could happen anytime. They all want to be top of mind when you suddenly decide, "Hey, I've got to get an auto insurance policy for that new car I'm buying!" Hence, the nonstop ads.

The bottom line is this: the seven systems of your business, like the systems in your car, need to be appropriate for the job they need to do, to work together seamlessly, to create greater efficiency, and to allow you, the owner, to drive your business and get the Business Mulligan you deserve, such as a Saturday afternoon with the family without your feeling as though you're letting the inmates run the asylum.

Key Concepts

- Systems affect each part of your business.
- Both marketing and workflow automation free you and your team to be more productive.
- Because businesses naturally become more complicated than necessary, you must intentionally simplify processes and systems.

Action Plan

Ask yourself these questions. If you answer yes to any of them, then *fix the problem*:

1. Do I have to tell my employees the same things over and over again?
2. When I leave the premises, does my business run off the rails?
3. When I hire someone new, do I have to invest hours of my time

training them?

4. If someone calls in sick, does their job go undone because no one else knows how to do it?

5. Does my business have a bunch of software programs and systems that are siloed and don't interface with each other, causing massive redundancy?

6. When I play eighteen rounds on a Saturday, am I incapable of enjoying myself because I'm worried about an employee screwing up at my business?

NINE

System 6: Administrative

How much?

How much do we keep?

More accurately—how much do we make, spend, risk, have, and keep?

If there's one thing I've learned about myself, and entrepreneurs in general, it's that we love creating things. We love dreaming, creating a vision, gathering resources, growing excitement and turning those dreams into reality. We love seeing the fruits of our labor realized — and once that's done, it's time to move on. For me, and I assume many entrepreneurs, the excitement is in the next thing.

I've also learned that I really don't like all the mundane responsibilities that come with the things I create: the day-to-day activities, the paperwork, billing, paying bills, regulations, licensing, insurance, accounting, and especially taxes. To some extent, I can credit this attitude with significant accomplishments over the years. Unfortunately, this attitude has also caused challenges, confusion, set backs and failures that did not have to happen had I simply made sure that the right things were being done while I set out to create and build.

Too Many Keys

Take a look at your key chain. Seriously. Take out your set of keys and try to identify every key and the lock it unlocks. You'll find the key to your home, maybe a key to your office, and depending upon how old your car is, you'll find a car key or a fob to unlock and drive it. Then, think about everything those keys actually represent. You may have a key that locks the gate that protects your property, keys to a filing cabinet that keeps your important documents secure, keys to your parents' house in case of emergencies.

If you have something that requires a key, it's your responsibility. With keys comes responsibility. And if you have too many keys, the associated responsibilities can add pressures and challenges that can become burdensome.

Can you have too many keys? Absolutely! Is it liberating to get rid of keys sometimes? You're dang right it is!

I remember buying my first home. It was a "starter home" and it needed a lot of work. It was only a little over a 1,200 square feet. Man, I was proud of that house. Over the first few years, I put a ton of work into it.

Four years later I had the opportunity to buy a small business in another city about an hour away. I didn't want to sell the house. Instead, I found a renter for the house before moving to the new city.

I was single at the time, so I got an apartment and became the landlord of my old house. Of course, as the owner, I maintained a key to the house in case of emergencies or if something needed to be done. No big deal—it was the same key, right? Yes and no. What that key now represented changed dramatically. The responsibilities of a landlord are remarkably different from those of a homeowner.

For example, when I owned the house and lived in it, I could postpone a repair if I wanted to. But as a landlord, when the tenant calls and says the disposal is not working, you need to either hustle over there yourself or hire someone to fix it. You can't put it off.

Over the next fifteen years, I added more and more keys to my keychain. I mean that literally and figuratively, of course. I had the new business, which later expanded into another city. I bought an eight-unit apartment complex and two additional rent houses. After getting married, my wife and I bought a new home. The keys and responsibilities simply kept adding up. More employees, more insurance, more accounting, more bills, more phone calls, more issues, more of everything—good and bad.

Having read this far in the book, you know where I'm headed. Yep—I became a slave to my keys.

Every time there was a problem, the guy with the key—me— had to drop everything and fix the problem. From clogged drains to bickering employees, I was Mr. Fixit. And, after a while, I began putting off the things I didn't enjoy doing because I viewed the things I did enjoy as higher priority.

What MUST Get Done?

Most likely we ask and answer that question daily. However, we likely look at it from two different perspectives: "What must get done?" or "What can we put off?" We each have our personal preferences and priorities, but we also have responsibilities. How could I continue acquiring, creating and building my dreams with all the noise the mundane stuff adds? The more we put off, the louder the noise gets.

One solution is to ignore those responsibilities. Another is to hire or train others to handle them. I believe that we all have strengths and talents. However, if we're lucky we are only great at one or two things. I know gifted salespeople who are terrible at paperwork. And, I know accountants that couldn't sell there way out of a paper bag. The same thing is true with business owners.

We all have our strengths and talents and priorities, but it's very risky to ignore other areas that we should be focused on. Again, we don't need to be the mechanic and fix every aspect of our businesses ourselves. We should, however, give the proper amount of attention to the administrative system. If this happens to be one of your weaknesses, as it is mine, ensure that these responsibilities are getting done so they don't cause unnecessary damage.

It's a No-brainer

This chapter is the shortest chapter in the book. It's not short because it's not important, but because it is a no brainer. If we continue putting off or ignoring our administrative responsibilities we will regret it. One day it will become the priority. And, it's sad when routine responsibilities cause damage to a good business.

Administrative responsibilities are everywhere in our businesses. Each system and each part of your business includes some sort of administrative duties. As business owners, we normally don't allow our team to shirk those duties, but, too often we excuse ourselves from deadlines. So, rather than letting those things build up give them their proper attention and ensure that they are done right the first time – whether you're the one doing it or not.

Don't allow your business to die because of something that didn't have to happen:

Pay your bills on time,

Pay your taxes on time,

Pay your people on time, every time,

Keep your bookkeeping up-to-date,

Get the proper certifications or licenses,

Make sure your insurance coverage is accurate and in place,

Manage from a budget,

Keep good employee records,

Document employee discipline and evaluations,

And, develop and operate from a business plan.

Look, this list could take up several pages. As I've said earlier, this book is not designed to cure every problem in your business. You have to identify the things you need to work on. The point I want to drive home is that administrative responsibilities always fall on the business owner. It's not your responsibility to physically do it, but it is imperative that you make sure it gets done right the first time and doesn't cause you unnecessary problems in the future. Usually administrative tasks aren't the strong suit of most entrepreneurs. But, as you've seen in this chapter, the efficiencies and profitability created by attending to administrative systems will free you from unnecessarily repeating work that could have been done once. This is time you could work on being the *most effective*. In the last of the seven systems, the personal system, we'll ask, "Where am I supposed to be right now?" The answer may surprise you.

> *Administrative systems will free you from unnecessarily repeating work that could have been done once.*

Key Concepts

- Recognize your talents and strengths and ensure others make up for your weaknesses..
- Ignoring administrative tasks doesn't kill your business quickly, but it can kill it eventually.
- Administrative responsibilities always fall on the business owner.

Action Plan

Explore how your company measures up to the following

administrative-related questions.

1. How quickly do you find out about something that has gone wrong in your business?

2. Are you often called upon to fix a problem that has been allowed to fester for too long?

3. Are each one of your administrative components—finance, human resources, marketing, operations, and planning—working as smoothly and efficiently as possible?

TEN

System 7: Personal

Where?

Where am I needed most right now?

Losing My Mind to My Business

As I sat on the hard bleachers to watch my boys, Ty and Matt, at their baseball game, I could see my daughter off to my right. Her mouth was moving, but I didn't know whom she was talking to or if she was actually talking at all. I literally couldn't hear a word she was saying. In fact, I couldn't hear any of the usual sounds from the ballpark: the pitches, the hits, the calls, or even the excited shouts of family members cheering on their sons. It was as if I had gone completely deaf.

Ann Marie was apparently asking me something, but my mind was somewhere else. It sure wasn't on the game either, because if someone had asked me what the score was I would have had to make it up.

Suddenly, I realized that Ann Marie was looking at me, and as my attention refocused, so did my hearing. It was like the volume was slowly being turned up on a radio. At first, it was a low sound and then seemed to be a yell: "Daddy . . . Daddy . . . Daddy . . .

115

DADDY!!!!"

"WHAT?!" I said as if she had just walked up to me and screamed in my face.

"Daddy, can I have a cool cup?" she asked.

As my consciousness crept back in, I realized that my body was in the stands but my mind was back at the office trying to figure out how in the world I was going to make payroll the next day. These thoughts had obliterated everything else.

Unfortunately, this began to happen more and more often: at dinner parties, at work, and even as I worshiped at church. I felt like I was losing my mind. In a way I guess I really was losing my mind to my business.

In this book I've presented and discussed six of the seven systems that comprise your business. All of them are equally important. Even with that said, this final system is the reason you're in business in the first place. It is why you need a Business Mulligan.

When you regain control of your business, you regain control of your life allowing you to work on all aspects of your life and keep your business in its proper perspective. When your business is in its proper perspective, you're most free to work on your business, instead of in it.

The personal system is the most challenging of the seven because it's all about you, the business owner. I don't just mean your qualifications, education, experience, or training; those are external attributes that can be acquired. I'm talking about you and your core attributes as a human being and business owner.

Since talking about and analyzing your personal system is, well, *personal*, I'll get the ball rolling by opening up about myself.

While I have accomplished a lot of things and done a lot of things, anyone can justifiably call me a dreamer, I dream up a lot more things than I end up doing. In fact, my wife once bought me a nicely framed quote, "We create our tomorrows by what we *dream* today." I loved it and still cherish the gift, but after years of dreaming and getting fewer things than I wanted accomplished, I began to question the theory. I think I bought into the dreaming part too much. One day I took out some white correction fluid and crossed out the word *dream* and replaced it with the word *do*. It still hangs in my office, but now reads, "We create our tomorrows by what we *do* today." That's where you get the rewards; it has nothing to do with the dream. It's only good if it comes true.

We Must Be People of Action

You're likely reading this book because your business has taken control of your life. If we can't control our business and it is controlling us, then we can't improve our relationships and our business determines our happiness, mood, and whether or not we are able to go on and accomplish other things in our lives. When things in our business are going badly, we do badly, and when things are going well, we do well. That is not the situation we want to be in. That is not what we bargained for.

This is a relationship shift. Right now, you feel as though you're not in charge of your life. Your business is running your life. The business has all the power in your relationship, and that makes it an unhealthy relationship.

We need to find the catalyst of change in our business that is going to allow us to make a shift whereby we regain control of our life. Like you, a big part of my life is my business; and just like part of my life is my relationships, part of my life is my health, but when something takes control, like a life-threatening illness, it takes control of me, so I cannot perform in other areas.

If you allow a disease or the illness to have control, it calls all the shots.

The exact same thing happens with your business. If you allow it to control your life, you can't make changes in the other areas of your life. Once you gain control and the business is serving you (as opposed to you serving it), then that's the mindset you need to have: you are the one in the driver's seat.

We all got into business to have control over how much money we make and how many hours we work. We also got into business to control the operations, and we feel like we know what's best because we feel like we can do it better than the competition or our old boss. And then we realize that the business we once dreamed of, or used to love, is not the business we have now.

Our customers are our bosses because they require changes or a service you hadn't thought of, or they demand that you deliver to them in a certain way. All of those changes are things you hadn't considered.

Your employees have demands. You think you hired the perfect person to work nights and weekends, and now they have a change in their life and announce, "Look, I've spent enough time working weekends and nights." They may deserve it, but that puts you back into a place where you're not in control, the employee is. It changes what you thought your ideal business was going to be because now you're doing what you think is required to make it work—you become the mechanic as opposed to the driver.

Like you, I'm willing to do or be anything for the business that's required to help it succeed and grow. Regardless of whether you're really good at that job, you're willing to do it for the sake of the business. And a few months down the road, you realize the business has control over you.

Though you want to regain control of your life, the business has got you pinned down. In my business, I was able to look deep into my business and identify something in our assets. I asked myself, "What can I do to make a change such that it improves the business and I'm able to shift or move talent or personnel around, and I'm able to reduce the number of people that we need?" I bought a software program that helped us automate both the marketing and the operations. When I put this program in, it completely changed our business.

In our situation, plugging that tool in allowed me to move talent and do more with fewer people because I was able to move people into the right positions. It improved productivity and perpetuated success. We were able to improve closure rates, we were able to market automatically, and it was repeatable. Not only did it save us time and money, but it helped increase sales and profits. Putting people in the right roles and seats freed me up to work on my business more, not just work in it.

Ultimately, in my business the marketplace demanded a significant business model shift. Several years after identifying that *control catalyst,* I realized that you may not need to change the business model to regain control, but you need to identify the one thing that when changed will change everything else. The decision I made helped me regain control of my business and regain perspective. I made the decision to regain control of my life, and I would regain control of my business, so it no longer controlled me; and then I was able to regain my health. By changing my perspective, I changed my life—that's where it made the shift.

Whether it's an injury, illness, or addiction, if something controls you or your life in one area, it's going to be very difficult to keep control in the other areas of your life. It's going to injure your relationships and your body. Whether it's alcoholism, cancer, or an unhealthy relationship, it controls you.

Remember the avatar for this book, Todd? He lost control of his life to his business, and nothing else is going to work very well until he is able to regain control of his life.

Todd is overwhelmed, but he thinks he's used to it. We need to help Todd identify why he got into business in the first place.

Control Catalyst

When I write, "control catalyst," what I mean is the place where you currently have the most leverage to affect your business. It's the one thing, out of the many things you can do, that will get you the most results.

To best understand it, let me give you an example: I have a coaching client named Roy. He is a counselor and has a very successful and personally fulfilling practice. However, as you may imagine, counseling can become emotionally draining, and after years of working one-to-one, he realized that he was trading hours for dollars. We took a long look at his business and tried to find things he could transform into digital products. He already did extensive speaking engagements and had created several popular three and four-day workshops where people would gladly stop what they were doing and attend live. He also had done a lot of videos and was really good at connecting with his market.

So, Roy set out to convert his workshops into online courses, and that is allowing him to scale his business as well as convert his one-to-one business into a one-to-many business. This was Roy's control catalyst. By identifying an area of his business that he had proven successful and finding a way to generate passive income through online courses and other digital products, Roy was able to see fewer clients and serve more people. This also freed him up to work on his business more than he was previously doing.

We all have an asset, thing, or person that can be the control catalyst. In your case, let's look at your business and find the one thing that can help get you out of "hours for dollars." And no doubt about it—take whatever it is—a book, a digital product, a course, a workshop—and turn it into a four- or five- or six-week online course that can serve many. If you focus on your control catalyst and decide it is going to get done, it's a good start to freeing you up to work more on your business.

I believe that every business that has been operating for a while has something or somebody that can be improved and, in doing so, can change the rest of your life or business. For instance, Roy's online courses, those were the catalyst that helped him begin the process of transforming his business to better serve his life.

We business owners are all experts at *something*. We've all worked 10,000 hours in something. Whether we love it or have a love-hate relationship with it, why not use that strength to be the control catalyst to start the process of regaining control of our lives?

We all go into business for the right reasons—to have control over our own destiny. We all love our business at first, but then we often end up having a love-hate relationship with it. Then we despise it some days while at the same time it's our baby and we want our baby to succeed and our name and reputation to go on and prosper.

That love-hate relationship has to change.

You have to love yourself *more* than you love your business.

When the business has control, it controls everything. Your health, sleep, diet, exercise—it's overwhelming to work on something.. This is the essence of the Business Mulligan.

Becoming a Business Owner

There are many words to describe you: entrepreneur, solopreneur, businessman or woman, CEO, president, and many others. I encourage you to begin seeing yourself as a *business owner*. I like this title because it declares a new and healthy relationship between you and your business. It says, "I own the business; the business doesn't own me." And that's a critical statement to yourself, your employees, customers, vendors, and the world.

That's why you got into business. You may not have used these words, but you wanted to be in control of your own destiny. You wanted out of a job working for a boss, and you wanted to make your unique contribution to the world, on your terms. You wanted the freedom from a schedule, and the financial rewards that come from owning a successful business. You wanted to be able to influence others, the marketplace, and the world. You wanted to change your lifestyle.

And then one day, you woke up and realized that the dream you had been pouring yourself into achieving was not a reality. The business might be successful in the moment, but your real dream of controlling your destiny, of freedom, and of lifestyle was not where you hoped it would be. You realized that your business was not serving you, but you were serving the business.

It's not worth owning a business if it owns you.

And this change to the business owning you is one that happens very slowly and often subtly.

To reverse this—start by identifying your control catalyst.

"It's Not Personal—It's Strictly Business."

In the classic 1972 film *The Godfather*, Al Pacino's character, Michael Corleone, said, "It's not personal, Sonny. It's strictly business."

> *It's not worth owning a business if it owns you.*

Decades later those immortal words have survived mostly intact and have been uttered by millions. You've heard it: "It's not personal, it's business." Baloney! If my business is on the line, you better believe it's personal to me. There are countless people who have heard those words right after they were fired or foreclosed upon.

"Sorry, Bill," the boss says as he hands Bill a pink slip. "It's not personal. It's a business decision."

In that moment, it becomes personal.

That's why this last of the seven areas is really the most important. Too many business owners believe they separate their businesses from their personal lives. To an extent you can, and should. If you're always taking your work stress home with you, it will mess up your home life, which will inevitably affect your business. That's why it's so important to see your business as being personal.

I'm not advocating that you identify your self-worth with your business. But I am suggesting that there's no value in pretending you don't have an emotional investment in your business. After all, you created it! This business is what feeds your family and pays your personal bills. It exists because you took time from your personal life to start it and keep it going. So it is personal. And that's okay.

Self-Made Men

You probably know a successful person whom everybody says is a "self-made" man. (Could be a "self-made" woman, too.) The idea is that this person raised themselves up by their own bootstraps, made their own way in the world, didn't get a boost from mommy or daddy, and achieved their fortune solely by the sweat of their own brow.

Hogwash. There is no such thing as a "self-made" man.

No matter who you are, there have been people at every stage of your personal and professional life who have been instrumental in helping you to become who you are, achieve what you've achieved, and do what you've done. This isn't to suggest they did it for you. But they helped you. You came into this world because of your parents. Since then there've been teachers, coaches, peers, friends, mentors, and others who have helped you.

I'd rather not go off on a tangent about all the people we have in our lives who support and encourage us. And, I'm sure you understand that without customers, no business could survive, much less thrive. But I simply can't believe that anyone who is considered "self-made" could have done anything without every single one of their teammates or employees helping to "make" them. Every person that I have ever been blessed to work with has helped me. And, I've learned from each person—some good stuff and some not so good, but I've learned from everyone.

Sure, you've taken plenty of risks. You've put yourself, your finances, and your reputation on the line for your business. You've gotten up early, worked late, and made other sacrifices to make your business work. No one can take that from you.

Yet if you are to continue to be successful, you cannot think of yourself as an island. This doesn't mean you don't take credit for what you've done; but when you spend some time thinking about who in your life has helped you to be where you are, then understand that power, it's liberating.

Throughout this book, I've mentioned that business owners need to drive their businesses. And, in the chapter entitled "Own It, Drive It," I suggest that business owners need to treat their businesses as if they were cars. It's such an easy analogy because you can't drive your car and change a flat tire at the same time, can you?

Now that you understand that your business is made up of seven systems and each system has individual parts, it's time to learn a simple step-by-step system to work on your business. In keeping with the car analogy, I'm going to teach you how to DRIVE FAR.

Key Concepts

- If your business owns you, it's not worth owning a business.
- Every day, ask yourself, "Where am I needed most right now?"
- Identify your control catalyst, the one thing you can do that will make the most difference in your business.

Action Plan

Think about the intersection of your personal life (that is, when you're not engaged in doing something for your business) and your business life.

- Is there a clear separation?
- The most obvious question is this: can you leave your business for a few days—or even two weeks—and not be stressed out about

what could go wrong? Can you go away without employees calling you while you're on the beach or at the game?

- If your answer is no, it means that your employees are constantly faced with situations for which they either 1) don't know the answer or 2) are afraid to make a decision. It's easier for them to call you.

- The solution to problem number 1 is training and systemization. The solution to number 2 is confidence and empowerment. It's also necessary that your employees know that if they do make a mistake or make a less-than-ideal choice, you're not going to criticize them, at least not in front of their colleagues.

- Make an effort to get your personal life under control along with your business. Don't be a victim! Drive your car—don't let it drive you.

ELEVEN

Drive Far

We've taken you from seeing your business as a whole to now, seeing it as individual parts of seven systems. This understanding alone, while giving you greater clarity, does not teach you *how* to work on your business. DRIVE FAR gives you the step-by-step process for working on your business.

DRIVE FAR—here's what it stands for:

Decide—I decide that I'm going to change the relationship I have with my business, and I'm going to work on my business.

Review—I'm going to review my business in its entirety and determine those systems that need my attention or focus.

Identify—I'm going to choose the single most important system that I'm committed to fix or repair.

Verbalize—I'm going to make sure the change is good and clear with regard to the team.

Execute—I'm going to ensure that decisions are transformed into action.

This last step consists of these three sub-steps (FAR):

Focus—I'm going to focus on what's needed.

Adjust—I'm going to make the necessary adjustments.

Replay—I'm going to replay the process to ensure it works.

A common mistake that business owners make is that we tend to look at our business in its totality. Of course, we all recognize the typical divisions, such as sales, marketing, finance, etc., but we still look at it as a whole, not the sum of its parts. The best way to see if you have been taking this perspective is to complete the exercise described at the end of this chapter, called the "Snapshot."

But, first take a ride with me.

Just like car owners, business owners do not need to be mechanics. We do not need to be experts in every area of our business. But we must stop looking at our businesses as the whole car. Our focus must be on those seven systems, their parts, and their component parts—which we've spent the seven previous chapters exploring in detail. It's the only way to know if something in our business is working optimally or not.

Like cars, businesses can run for quite a while with parts that need repair or replacement. Cars and businesses can sometimes run without major parts. No car runs optimally unless we know which parts are needed and/or are in need of repair or replacement. It's simple and eye-opening when we take inventory of all of the parts of our business. Since we've addressed the seven systems of a business in such detail, you have a listing of the key elements to take this inventory.

Now that you are out from under the hood and in the driver's seat, you can see the road ahead and read the gauges of your various systems.

To orient yourself to the process, please look at the seven columns <u>in the "Snapshot" graphic located</u> at the end of the chapter. Each column is an area of focus. You'll notice that each column contains two columns of boxes. On the left side, the boxes will be filled in with the names of each part in your business. On the right side, you'll list any component parts involved with the particular part. Please draw a line from the part to each component part connecting the two.

Beside each box are three letters: R, Y, and G. These letters are the first letter in the colors red, yellow, and green, indicative of traffic lights. In our worksheet, it is a system of measurement and coincides with your assessment of whether or not the part is working optimally (green – G), needs repair (yellow – Y), or needs replacement (red – R).

Once completed, this exercise will serve you well as you begin to focus on the areas of your business that need the most attention. If used as a "Snapshot," it will also serve to show how your efforts are paying off.

It's important that you first concentrate on the parts of your business you have in place now, not what you hope to have in the future. Again, this is a picture of where your business is today. We'll work toward adding other parts as we begin to regain more control.

Decide

The first decision is to take the business owner's perspective. This is a mindset shift. Rather than me walking in my business, turning the lights on, and going about the day trying to survive, I go in with the intention to improve the business. Then I commit to working on something for one solid week or a month or two months. It's the commitment to the decision. And, it's the decisions that really change our lives.

While oftentimes we need to hear ourselves say something before we can believe it enough to commit to doing it, it's critical to actually decide rather than just say something. Many think they decide on something even when they're really just contemplating the decision. When you say, "I'm going to lose weight," it's one thing to *say* it and another thing to *do* it.

For example, I'm the kind of person who thinks of new business ideas. I think of a business idea and proceed to say to myself, "I'm going to do it!" Then I'll need to flesh out in my mind whether it's a good idea or not. Often, I'll share that idea with people, and they'll respond, "Yeah, that's a good idea," which tells me I have a good idea and that reinforces my contemplating. But that's not a decision.

You may have an idea to write a book. Easier said than done. It's very hard to finish writing a book. In fact, eighty-five percent of people who say they're going to write a book never do. While it's easy to start, finishing it—heck, even getting past the first chapter—is much harder than most people think.

The point is: we're going to face unexpected challenges and obstacles. Deciding means that you've considered the difficulty, identified some of the potential obstacles and challenges, and know that some will crop up and surprise you; but you will do what it takes to overcome them to achieve your goal. Deciding means that you're committed to actually doing it regardless of the challenges, obstacles, or excuses that arise or that you conjure up.

If you're like me, maybe it's your perfectionism that becomes an obstacle. Maybe you want to become a business owner but deep down you know it's going to be messy and hard, and you won't be able to do it perfectly. Maybe it's your need for control, that if you move into the role of business owner, you'll lose control, and you fear losing your business along with it. Deciding means facing your fears, obstacles, excuses, and anything else that comes between you and your goal. Deciding is making a commitment to deal with them as they come up, to do whatever it takes to overcome them, ease them, sidestep them, and move through them. When you decide, it's set in stone.

Deciding means that you're committed to actually doing it regardless of the challenges, obstacles, or excuses that arise or that you conjure up.

You've done this. Think back to some of the things you've accomplished so far in life. Think back to your successes. The fact that you currently own a business is a huge success. You may not realize it, but you had to overcome many obstacles, challenges, and excuses to do that. You had to decide, commit, and throw yourself into it. And look what happened—you did it.

Don't let this be another thing you say you're going to do and then not follow through. All of those unfinished items don't just go away. They build up and eat at us when we're not thinking about them. They sap the vital energy and focus we need to be business owners. Those things most likely didn't happen because you didn't make a firm decision. You *wished* for them to happen, probably *wanted* them to happen, but you never *decided* to make them happen—*no matter what*. Deciding means making up your mind and being committed to a result. The word "decide" and the letter D in our acronym mean: a decision must be made that you are going to work on a particular system or part of your business. That's a decision.

Just begin by saying, "I'm going to improve this week." We're so busy that it can be hard to find the part of your business that you need to work on. You're in the business. You're underwater busy, and it's hard to find the one thing you need to be working on. Rather than saying, "I'm going to turn the lights on and go about my day and allow other peoples' agendas to run the day, instead of me driving the day," instead say, "I'm going to fix something. I'm going to solve some problems."

Review

Look at the seven systems of your business. Rate them and their parts, and determine if they need replacing, repair, or if they are running optimally. Can they be improved? There are some parts that you may need to add and some that can be left alone.

From an owner's perspective you can do an overall review. This is a broad view in order to identify and prioritize what you need to fix. You have to take an owner's perspective. Even if the business is working okay, you may need to add a marketing piece, for example.

Review how each system has operated and whether it needs repair or replacement. When you're reviewing and looking at your business deeper than its totality and you've identified a system that needs repair, then you can review how it was set up originally and how it functions today, and then set goals for how you think it should operate in that system. The review process is critical because you have to determine whether a part needs replacement or repair, or if it's running well enough to deal with later. Even if it's not optimal today, but it's functioning well enough, you can focus on something that needs your attention.

Identify

After reviewing all the systems and committing to improve one part of one system, it's time to name the part that you will focus on. This process allows you to hone in on the specific part that needs attention, so you can determine if the part needs replacing or repair. This will also allow you to estimate who will do the repairs and how they will take place. Further estimations will be made as you begin discussing proposed repairs with your team.

Fires are going to appear. At first, your business is going to tell you where they are.

Where are your pain points?

Where are your weaknesses?

What are the complaints?

What's been aggravating you as the owner for a while?

It's important that you take yourself out from under the hood and get back in the driver's seat. You are a business owner now, not a highly paid employee. Once you make this paradigm shift, you'll see the parts that need work.

Verbalize

As I've mentioned before in discussing the system of culture, the support of your team is critical to your Business Mulligan—getting them to see what's going on and what they need to improve. If you can engage your team members and get them to gain ownership by simply being a part of the solution, then they will also gain some experience by being part of the solution. It can also spur their own creativity to solve problems. Every bit of that will free you up as the owner to either take time off or focus on another part of the business.

You can't do this without the buy-in and trust of your team.

Talk with your team and key players about making adjustments. Discuss the pros and cons of making adjustments. Working on your business requires support from your team. You explain that you're trying to take the business to a better place for everyone's benefit, and that because the economy is changing so quickly, in order for the business to stay open and thrive, you all must make a shift. And to do things differently, you need your team's help to move in that direction.

One business owner was about to close the doors to his business after thirty years. He told his employees that he was going to have to shut down. One of his employees said, "You had my hands for thirty years. You could have had my mind, but you never once asked me what I thought about the company." Remember: two heads are better than one.

In collaborating with your team, you're getting a different perspective, and it's going to improve things. Ultimately, it is your business, you are responsible, and your decisions determine your success. So you've got to communicate to your employees that as much as you appreciate their assistance and you will always listen to them, you may not take their advice every time.

Because we have the long-range approach, we have a system in place, and we'll keep working at it until we get it right.

Look at your employees from a different perspective. Involve them in transforming the business. Looking deeply into these systems, the team will play a big part in transforming the business for long-lasting success. Once you get the buy-in from the team, it both compounds your expertise, and they get to play a bigger part. Everyone wins!

Execute = FAR

The "FAR" in DRIVE FAR is the execution. You'll *focus*, *adjust*, and *replay*. You do that until you get it right.

Ideas are cheap. Execution is everything. Once you've done all this stuff and you know the direction you want to head in, it's time to execute.

Let's say you decide that in order to improve the conversion system, you want to set up a landing page. You need to make sure you have the right tools. You want to use the best practices for conversion, so you have to employ a designer. Whatever it takes for the particular part you're working on, you need to set it in action. You need to make a goal, put it on a timeline, and see it through to completion.

One of the most important parts of that is learning that *done* is better than *great*. While it can become great as you continue to *focus*, *adjust*, and *replay*, if you never complete it and it's never out there, your business cannot be improved upon, and your business can become stagnant. *Done is better than great.*

I speak from experience. When I was writing this book, I had the hardest time finishing it because I wanted it to be perfect. But perfection, at least in a book, can never be achieved. You can always write another paragraph or add another example! At some point you just have to determine, "Okay, this is it. I'm done."

> *Done is better than great.*

The FAR system will allow you to revisit a project and improve upon it when you decide it needs to be worked on again.

Focus

You're a decider.

Think back to the days leading up to your starting a business. There was at least one point when you made a decision. That decision may have been to leave your job, buy into your company, strike out on your own, and turn your idea into reality. You made up your mind to take action. Your ability to make decisions—often big decisions where the outcome was uncertain—has been a critical asset of yours that has gotten you to this point.

But with more success comes more responsibility. When there was less to lose, decisions not working cost you less. When we're starting out, if we haven't tasted success yet, we aren't afraid to lose what we don't have or don't know. Today that's different. Your ability to decide, make difficult choices, and manage the outcomes is hampered by a dizzying array of options. There are times in business when everything calling for our attention is critical. This can lead us to decision paralysis. We never focus because we never decide where our focus is needed most.

Focus only on the part that needs repair or replacement. John Lee Dumas, founder and host of the podcast "Entrepreneur on Fire," often uses the acronym FOCUS, which stands for *Follow One Course Until Success*. This means that as you focus on the part of your business that needs repair, do not shift your focus anywhere else until you have met your goals with this part. Otherwise, you can be drawn into that other shiny object and never really attend to what needs repair or fixing.

You can waste so much time getting through the day that you don't accomplish anything that moves you forward. It's hard to improve when you're doing nothing but fixing small problems that keep popping up like whack-a-moles. You whack, whack, whack all day long, and still—they keep coming! Do yourself a favor: stay focused on the most important problem that needs fixing.

Adjust

Make small, calculated adjustments to the parts in your focus. Like a golf swing, you either are going to feel it, know it, or have evidence that you need to adjust on your next opportunity. For example, in a golf swing, if the ball goes left, you know that you need to open the face more and hit it more squarely. In your business, you will likely to know the adjustments that need to occur to improve a given part. Avoid massive adjustments because you want to remain focused on your outcome and what the parts are supposed to do.

For example, say you're looking at an advertising piece. You massively adjust it, and it either slows down your leads completely or it increases your leads so dramatically that you can't handle the business. One result is that your leads dry up, so you don't have business. Alternatively, if you make a huge adjustment and you have more leads than you can handle, then you overload your operations and they're not able to deliver. You risk injuring your reputation, which ultimately will cause you to lose business. Therefore, small, continuous adjustments with improved results are what you should set out to do.

Replay

I was deliberate when I chose to use the word replay. I tried several other words that worked well, but had different meanings. I tried; redo, repair, repeat. Each worked, but only replay explains what I want you to do. We certainly don't want to repeat what we've already done. If a golfer to a mulligan and just repeated his last shot, he'd be upset. Instead, after focusing on the shot, then making the proper adjustments he replays the shot. That's what I want you to do. Focus on a part of you business that isn't working optimally; make the proper adjustments and replay, until it's right. Then, move on to the next part that needs your attention.

The "Snapshot"

We've all seen the ads for weight-loss companies where they show "before" and "after" pictures. I have to admit that these pictures always made quite an impression on me; and they must work well for the companies because they keep advertising that way. It also reminds me of all the times I wrap up projects around the house and regret not having taken "before" pictures. You don't want to go too far down the road without being able to enjoy results from hard work. Taking your "Snapshot" now will allow you a valuable point of comparison at any point in the future.

My hope is that the DRIVE FAR process gives you a system to work on each part of your business, giving you more freedom and control, which is your Business Mulligan. Like I said at the beginning of the book, it doesn't happen overnight. Trust me, you'll get frustrated along the way, and there will be times you're going to need a reminder of how far you've come. Hold on to your "Snapshots" along the way. Looking back on them and comparing them to future "Snapshots" will give you a clear reminder of how far you've come.

It's going to take hard work and focus to remove you from your day-to-day activities. But as you begin to implement the Mulligan Method, using the simple DRIVE FAR process, you will find that one day, you are in the driver's seat of a business that serves you, rather than you serving it.

Use the illustration below as a template for your "Snapshot" or visit businessmulligan.com/snapshot to print your "Snapshot" Worksheet.

Key Concepts

- Understanding your business is not the same as working on your business.
- It's important to involve your team as much as possible in the DRIVE FAR process.

Action Plan

Since this chapter is nothing more than a massive Action Plan, I'm going to ask you to enact the DRIVE FAR system. It begins with your decision to break free of the chains that bind you to your business, and from there you will establish a new relationship to your business. Once you've done this, then get to work!

Also make sure to take a "Snapshot" of your business as it is right now, so you can have a "before" shot. It will provide an easy measure to show how far you've progressed since you embraced the Mulligan Method—a great motivator to build on that progress too!

Remember that just like losing weight, it's not going to happen overnight. What you're looking for is consistent and steady progress. Take it step by step, and don't turn back!

CONCLUSION: PUTTING THE MULLIGAN METHOD INTO ACTION

Books are funny things. Sometimes we buy them and although we have every intention to read them, we never quite get around to it. Or, we'll start them and life gets in the way and they end up on the bookshelf with all the other books we'll get to. So, if you're reading this conclusion, you're either reading the book from cover to cover or you've skipped ahead. Either way, thanks for being here.

I'll give a quick recap and get straight into how you can put the Mulligan Method to work.

Our businesses mirror the world. When times were simpler, running a business was simpler. Today, technology is changing the way business is done. We're living in one of the most exciting times in the history of the world. But, technological advances are occurring so rapidly, it's hard to keep up and even harder competing in the business world.

The smartphone is changing how we communicate with each other, how we shop and buy products; it's even changing how we live. I went to a doctor's appointment the other day and the waiting room was full of people, from 8 to 80. All I could see was the top of their heads as they stared into the phones.

As business owners, we continue trying new technology, in our small businesses. Unfortunately, most of the time we find that we're just adding layers of complexity, confusion and chaos. And, we're becoming overwhelmed because we're being pulled deeper and deeper into the trenches of our businesses because of our willingness to do anything to survive.

We've all heard the expression, "Work ON your business, not IN your business." That's good and fine, but in this rapidly changing world HOW do we work on our business?

The Mulligan Method helps you look at your business from a different perspective: in systems and parts, not just your business as a whole. Similar to a car, your business is made up of systems and those systems contain parts.

If your car breaks you'll likely acknowledge that you need a mechanic to fix it. Most likely, you can tell that something is wrong and you might even have a good idea of what is broken. But, unless you're a mechanic, you'll need someone to help you fix you car so you can get back to your life.

Your mechanic will first focus on the affected system, and then he'll look at the parts that make up that system. To fix it, he must determine whether to repair the part or replace it. That's it.

Now, the difference in your business is that you have gotten used to being the mechanic. It's a very normal and very predictable problem – especially because of the complexities of business today. This has to stop!

We're finding ourselves in unhealthy relationships with our businesses. Too often we feel more like our business owns us rather than we own our businesses.

Two key points: You are the driver of your business. You are not a mechanic.

Here are the systems of your business and the questions each system asks:

1. *Attraction* – Who? Who is our ideal customer?
2. *Conversion* – When? When do we ask for the sale?
3. *Delivery* – What? What value do we provide?
4. *Systems* – How? How do we operate profitably?
5. *Culture* – Why? Why do we do what we do?
6. *Administrative* – How much? How much do we keep?

7. *Personal* – Where? Where am I most needed right now?

As you set out to work on your business more than you work in it, you'll want to focus on the systems that need the most attention. In order to identify the problems, you'll need to look at the parts within the systems. I have created a worksheet called the "Snapshot" to list the parts within each system. It's important to identify each part individually and understand why that part exists. As the owner, you'll need to determine if it needs repair, replacement or if the business needs other repairs more.

To help you determine which parts to work on, use the DRIVE FAR process.

Decide—I'm going to work on my business.

Review—I'm going to review my business in its entirety and determine those systems that need my attention or focus.

Identify—I'm going to choose the single most important system that I'm committed to fix or repair.

Verbalize—I'm going to make sure the change is good and clear with regard to the team.

Execute—I'm going to ensure that decisions are transformed into action.

This last step consists of these three sub-steps (FAR):

Focus—I'm going to focus on what's needed.

Adjust—I'm going to make the necessary adjustments.

Replay—I'm going to replay the process to ensure it works.

By looking at your business in systems and parts you'll begin to gain more clarity about what needs to be done in your business. As you begin working on your business more than you work in it, you'll start to regain more control. Your team will soon see a change in you and they will gain ownership by being a part of the solution. This further frees you up to work on your business more.

That's your Business Mulligan. But, it shouldn't stop with you.

You'll want to share the Mulligan Method with every member of your team. Start by employing this yourself, from the business owner perspective. Then, when you are consistently applying DRIVE FAR to work on your business share it with your key members. For example, your Sales Manager is responsible for converting leads into sales, right? She too can take a "Snapshot", because the seven systems apply in the sales department, too. She must attract new leads, convert them into sales and ensure that they are satisfied. Her department contains systems, culture, administrative responsibilities and she certainly needs to focus on a personal level. Every department contains the seven systems.

Finally, every team member, in every department should apply DRIVE FAR in their roles.

Work with your leaders, managers and team members on their systems and parts. Show them how to look at their roles from a different perspective. Teach them how to Focus, Adjust and Replay - until they get it right.

ABOUT THE AUTHOR

Jeff Martin

Founder of Business Mulligan, a community one hundred percent dedicated to helping business owners own their lives, Jeff Martin is a business growth expert who has created and owned several successful businesses, which range from real estate holdings to paramedical examination firms.

Jeff was on the forefront of the DNA testing market and successfully navigated many challenges and industry changes as the market exploded in the late 1990s. These market changes forced several significant business model shifts, which were, at times, complicated and painful, but necessary for survival. His most recent venture was a nationwide DNA relationship testing company, which was named one of the fastest growing franchises as well as being listed in the Top 100 new franchises in its first year by *Franchise Market Magazine*.

A veteran of the United States Navy, Jeff served as a Fleet Marine Force Corpsman to a Marine Corps artillery unit during Operations Desert Shield and Desert Storm. Jeff credits his combat experience for his leadership skills and the tenacity required to survive the ups and downs that come with being an early adopter in a new market. He is also a graduate of the E. J. Ourso College of Business at Louisiana State University.

Jeff coaches business owners on organizing and growing their companies, and creating and launching digital products. He is an Infusionsoft Certified Partner and an expert in marketing and workflow automation. He lives with his wife Katie and their three children in Lafayette, Louisiana. He is active in his church and serves on a committee for the Boy Scouts of America.